Clan Walk Guides

Walking
The Trossachs,
Loch Lomondside
and the
Campsie Fells

Mary Welsh
and
Christine Isherwood

First Published by Clan Books 2005

ISBN 1 873597 21 5
Text and Illustrations
© Mary Welsh
and
Christine Isherwood
2005

Clan Books
Clandon House
The Cross, Doune
Perthshire
FK16 6BE

Printed by
Cordfall Ltd, Glasgow

Walking
The Trossachs, Loch Lomondside
and the Campsie Fells

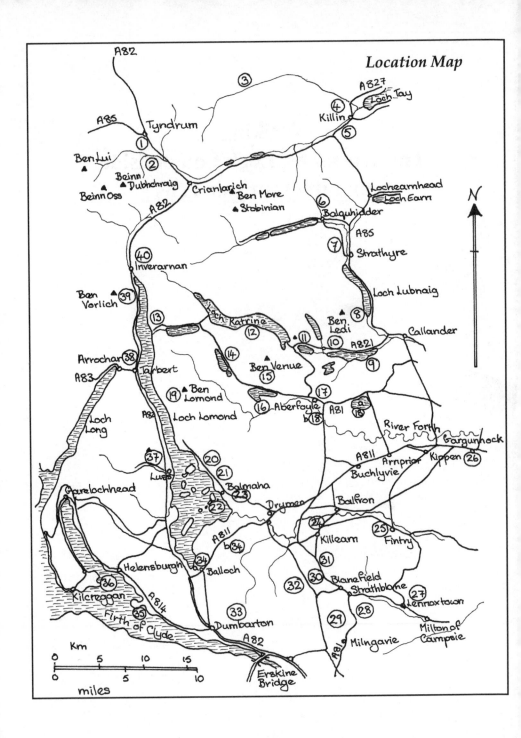

Contents

Contents continued page 4

Authors' Note

Please remember on all these walks:
   Wear suitable clothes and take adequate waterproofs.
   Walk in strong footwear; walking boots are advisable.
   Carry the relevant map and know how to use it.
   Take extra food and drink as emergency rations.
   Carry a whistle; remember six long blasts repeated at one
   minute intervals is the distress signal.
   Do not walk alone, and tell someone where you are going.
   If mist descends, return.
   Keep all dogs under strict control. Observe all 'No Dogs'
   notices—they are there for very good reasons.
Readers are advised that while the authors have taken every
effort to ensure the accuracy of this guidebook, changes can
occur after publication. You should check locally on transport,
accommodation, etc. The publisher would welcome notes of
any changes. Neither the publisher nor the authors can accept
responsibility for errors, omissions or any loss or injury.
   We also wish to record grateful thanks to Jennifer
Outhwaite for her help in the preparation of this volume.

Tyndrum and Cononish Glen

Park in the car park just north of the Tourist Information Centre at Tyndrum, grid ref 328304. This lies on the west side of the A82.

Tyndrum is surrounded by some of the finest mountains in the southern highlands. Ben Lui, with its cone-shaped top, is perhaps the most eye-catching. Its high slopes and corries are noted for alpine plants as exciting to botanists as its slopes are to walkers.

Scotland has limited **gold deposits** some of which were used in the Scottish Honours (crown jewels). Tyndrum was known as Scotland's gold capital. In the nineteenth century it was the scene of a short-lived goldrush. More recently Tyndrum's gold mine at Cononish was reopened. Another heavy metal, lead, was at the root of the development of village. Sir Robert Clifton discovered lead ore in 1741 and it was mined continuously until 1862 and briefly in the twentieth century. He gave his name to the tiny hamlet of Clifton, now part of Tyndrum, which was built to house the miners.

Fillan the missionary was a traveller on foot in the strath between Tyndrum and Killin. He came to the area to spread the teachings of the Christian way of life

Carved stone near Tyndrum

5

to the Scots and the Picts having travelled from Ireland with his mother and uncle. He settled in the glen while his relatives moved to another part of the country. Following his death he was made a saint because of his loving care for the area and its people. Among the trees near Kirkton farm, a priory was built in his memory.

Walk 1

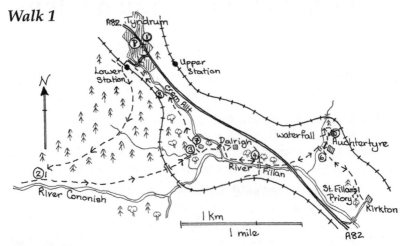

1. Turn right out of the car park, go past the toilets and turn right into Lower Station Road. Follow the road as it winds right, and then left, to come to the railway line, which you cross with care and ignoring the 'private' notices, using the white kissing gates. Walk on winding left and gently climbing a wide track signed, Cononish and Ben Lui. The way passes through an extensive conifer plantation, then levels and you can enjoy the view ahead. As the path begins to descend and wind a little you have a splendid view of Ben Lui with its cone-shaped summit. Go through a gate in the deer fence across the track, to leave the trees behind. Walk on into the open valley of the River Cononish to come to a T-junction. Pause here and look right to see Cononish farm, with the gold mine above.

2. Walk left along another wide track, which runs parallel with the river. Rough pastures slope down, right, to the burn, and beyond, more rough pastures slope up towards Beinn Dubhchraig. Here you might spot a kestrel hovering above the pasture. Then from the path you can see, over to the right, native Scots pine, nicely spread over the hill slopes. Follow the track as it moves in among a series of drumlins, glacial mounds. Go on under a railway bridge

which carries the Oban branch of the West Highland railway line. Step over a cattle grid and carry on with deciduous woodland to the left and steep bracken slopes to the right. The track then moves in among more drumlins, where a tall hummock has been planted with rowan and birch. On top of the mound is a sculpture depicting the phases of the moon.

3. Go on to join the West Highland Way (WHW), which here turns left, north, and is your return route. But, in order to visit a splendid waterfall and the remnants of St Fillan's priory, carry on, ahead (east), along the WHW. Cross a cattle grid and walk on along a lovely stretch of the long distance route. At the Y-junction, take the left branch to come to a wooden bridge over the Crom Allt, where the pretty tree-lined burn races over its rocky bed. A few steps on, wind right as directed by the WHW marker. Stroll on along the valley, with the river idling to your right. Soon you come to the 'Field of Dal Righ'. It was here in 1306, MacDougall of Lorne and his men were pursuing Robert Bruce's force who threw their heaviest weapons into a small lochan, hoping to escape. They were caught but managed to fight and kill MacDougall's men.

4. Continue on through birch to continue to a 'dead-end' road, the former main road. Cross and continue along the WHW beside the river, now named the Fillan. It was here that St Fillan carried out baptisms in the Holy Pool. Walk the delightful way to come to the A82, which you cross with the greatest of care. Stroll on along the WHW, now a metalled road, leading to Auchtertyre farm. The road brings you to a barn and then winds right across a bridge over the Auchtertyre Burn. Once over, turn left and walk up the slope, passing the 'wigwams' on the left. These are small 'pods' which provide inexpensive accommodation for walkers on WHW.

5. Just beyond the 4th pod, turn left and follow the sign for 'Woodland walk'. Keep ahead under pine to descend steps to cross a side stream and then wind, right, up a path, railed on the left, where the burn descends

Kestrel

7

in great fury through its deep ravine. Continue up the slope and wind left with the rails and pause to enjoy the fine waterfall. Follow the path round inside the woodland, soon to descend beside the small stream to return to the sign, seen earlier. Join the track, turn right and walk on to rejoin the WHW.

6. Turn left to pass the farm's outbuildings and the facilities for the campers and walk out into the strath. Follow the pleasing gated way through the fertile pastures, with good views ahead. Just before Kirkton farm and a small cemetery stand, on the right, the remains of St Fillan's church, almost hidden from sight by a copse of mature sycamore. After a pause in this charming corner, retrace your steps to Auchtertyre farm. Cross the bridge and wind left to walk to the side of the A-road. Cross, with care, and carry on along the WHW to re-walk your outward route until you reach the well signposted turn on the right.

7. The narrower way climbs gently to pass a lochan, where, perhaps, Robert the Bruce and his men tossed their heaviest weapons. There are two seats here with carvings on them. Follow the lovely way as it continues, winding between drumlins, covered with cushions of heather and scattered birch, with the Crom Allt to your right, meandering through the valley bottom. As you near a deer gate that leads into mixed woodland, look right, to see an extensive area of bare ground, where lead ore was brought down from the mines in the hills. Here it was crushed and smelted and the ingots sent by packhorse to Alloa, 50 miles away.

8. Go through the kissing gate, walk on to take the signposted way through pines to come close beside the river. At Lower Station Road, walked earlier, turn right and at the A-road, turn left to return to the parking area.

Practicals

Type of walk: A very pleasing walk on good clear tracks and paths through delightful countryside. Families should take great care crossing the A82 at point 4.

Distance:	7 ½ miles/12km
Time:	3–4 hours
Maps:	OS Explorer 364, OS Landranger 50.

Coille Coire Chuilc

Park in the good car park, grid ref 344292, for Tyndrum community woodland, at Dalrigh, on the left side of the road travelling from Crianlarich to Tyndrum. This is reached from the A82 at about 1 mile south-east of Tyndrum.

The pinewood, **Coille Coire Chuilc,** is a particularly beautiful remnant of the ancient Caledonian pinewoods, which once covered all the ground here. Notice the splendid ancient pines, and also younger regenerating trees which give hope for the future continuance of the wood.

You will notice **two railways** going up the valley below you. Nowadays they join at Crianlarich but run separately through Tyndrum, one going to Oban and the other to Fort William. They were built by different (rival) railway companies and crossed but did not join at Crianlarich for many years.

Coille Coire Chuille and Ben Chuirn

Walk 2

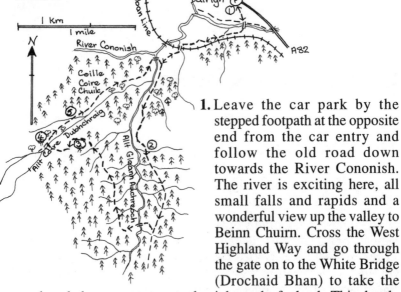

1. Leave the car park by the stepped footpath at the opposite end from the car entry and follow the old road down towards the River Cononish. The river is exciting here, all small falls and rapids and a wonderful view up the valley to Beinn Chuirn. Cross the West Highland Way and go through the gate on to the White Bridge (Drochaid Bhan) to take the good track that curves away to the right on the far bank. This shortly meets the Oban railway and runs for a while beside it. Notice the splendid array of moraine deposits between the track and the river, left behind when the glacier melted. Follow the track across the railway bridge and on towards the ancient pine forest with Beinn Dubhchraig behind it. The views are splendid. As the track comes round above the river, the Allt Gleann Auchreoch, look back down to the right to see a bridge and notice a clear path crossing towards the higher ground of the river terrace; this is your return path. The outward track remains above the Allt Gleann Auchreoch, with the main body of the pine forest on the far side although there are some spectacular old pines to be seen on both sides.

2. Continue along the pleasant track, where you might spot fox droppings, ignoring a wooden bridge leading into the pines. After a while you reach a decrepit deer fence with a locked gate and the start of a conifer plantation. The fence just above the track is very broken and is clearly the standard means of entry: cross it with care and return to the track as it winds gently through the spruce. There are plenty of breaks in the trees which afford excellent views up to Beinn Dubhchraig. At the track junction take the right turn, leading sharply back and downhill. Soon the way curves round to

the left, crosses the river on a wooden bridge and heads uphill. Enjoy the lovely views across to Beinn Odhar and Beinn Dorain behind Tyndrum as the track leads you up through the plantation. There are both pine marten and fox droppings on the track. Look out for these secretive mammals, you may be lucky enough to catch a glimpse.

3. Very soon the track starts to climb more steeply; follow it as it ascends round a hairpin bend and then flattens out again. Shortly afterwards you reach a turning circle and the end of the track. Here take a small footpath which continues on towards the Allt Coire Dubhchraig and the clear footpath on its far side. The river is fairly easy to cross on stones at the point where a small tributary enters on the far bank.

4. Once across the river turn right to follow the path which continues downstream close beside it. At the Y-junction take the left branch which moves away from the river a little. Follow it round until it joins another larger path coming in on your left. Turn right along this and continue downhill. Admire the spectacular waterfall on the main river to the right. From here the path leads down between the scattered birch of the river valley and small planted conifers. It may be boggy in winter or after heavy rain so you will have to pick your way in places.

5. Shortly after crossing a small stream you reach a deer fence; climb the high stile and continue down the path as it leads through birch. There is a beautiful dead pine over to the left, which marks the beginning of the superb ancient Caledonian pine forest, called Coille Coire Chuilc. The footpath winds its way among the fine old trees. The second deer fence is, at the time of writing, broken and the stile is surrounded on both sides by bog. There are several

Fox

11

large holes in the fence, clearly used regularly by walkers: make your way through one of these and follow the main path down a clear ridge through the centre of the forest, keeping to the higher and drier ground away from the river bank. Come down to the riverside just downstream of the confluence between the Allt Gleann Auchreoch and the Allt Coire Dubhchraig. Continue along the riverbank to a footbridge over the Allt Gleann Auchreoch, just before it joins the River Cononish. Cross and turn half right to climb a path up the river terrace (the one you noted on your outward route). Rejoin the track at the top and turn left to cross the railway bridge and return to the car park.

Buzzard

Practicals

Type of walk: Paths all the way. The track which goes most of the way is old and good, giving comfortable walking; the climbing is gradual. The path down is well used by Munro climbers and at the time of writing is seriously in need of repair in places. If the rivers are in spate after heavy rain the ford on the Allt Coire Dubhchraig may be difficult to cross. You should bear this in mind before starting the walk. Normally it should not be a problem.

Distance: 6 ½ miles/10.5km
Time: 3–4 hours
Maps: OS Explorer 364, OS Landranger 50

Glen Lochay

Park in the large space at the end of the metalled road just beyond Kenknock, grid ref 466365. To reach this use either of the minor roads which leave the A827 either side of the River Lochay just north of Killin.

Glen Lochay is a short but beautiful glen, the centre of the old hunting forest of Mamlorn. Its wooded lower reaches soon give way to the lonely, relatively remote upper glen, where this walk is set. It is the start of the climb to five Munros. It is bleak on a dull day but, in good weather, the views in both directions and the sense of isolation make this walk thoroughly enjoyable.

Glen Lochay and Ben Challum

1. Walk straight ahead from the car park to cross a bridge and on through a gate. The track, which is old and pleasant to walk, runs along the river bank and under a huge pipe, part of the local hydro scheme. Where the path forks take the right branch which leads away from the river towards a barn on the hillside. Go through the gate beside the barn and wind round hummocks of moraine before coming downhill to the riverbank once more. At the head of the

13

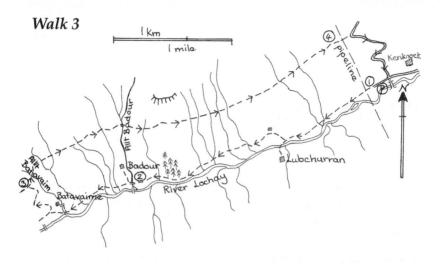

glen you can see dramatic Ben
Challum. The track winds
round between a stand of conifers and the river. Dippers
frequent this fast upland burn
and buzzards soar over the surrounding hillsides. To your right
is bulky Beinn Heasgarnich
with the more interesting
rocky spurs of Creag Mhor
beyond towards the head
of the glen. Across the
river are first Sgiath
Chuil and then
Meall Glas, both
rather undistin-
guished from this
side. In autumn
deer wander the
lower slopes and
the roaring of the
stags is with you
all day.

Red deer stag

14

2. Go along the track below the farm buildings of Badour and on towards the cottage at Batavaime. Go up, right, towards the dwelling to go across the bridge over the Allt Batavaim. Once over, the track curves round and begins to climb the hillside towards one of the spurs of Creag Mhor—Sron nan Eun (the bird's nose). At a fork take the right branch which zigzags gently on uphill. There is an obvious old spoil heap ahead and above this your track joins a hydro track.

3. Turn right and, after a little climbing, the way contours along the side of the glen. Continue on the easy way, crossing the many burns by bridges. The views down the glen are splendid, towards Meall nan Tarmachan and the fertile flat bottomed Glen Lochay with deciduous woods on either side and in the distance a glimpse of Loch Tay. Go through a gate and carry on along the high level way.

4. Eventually you come to another spoil heap and then cross the pipeline. There is a locked gate across the track beyond this point so you will have to climb the wooden fence beside it to reach the tarred hydro road from Kenknock over to Glen Lyon. Turn right and descend the zigzags to return to the parking space.

Practicals

Type of walk: An easy walk on tracks all the way, with splendid views in good weather. For deer shooting information (26 Aug–20 Oct), use Glen Dochart and Glen Lochay Hillphones Service (recorded message) 01567 820886.

Distance: 7 ½ miles/12km
Time: 3–4 hours
Maps: OS Explorer 378, OS Landranger 51

4

Sron a'Chlachain from Killin

Killin has several car parks. This walk starts from one at grid ref 573326. To access this, if coming from the south by the A827, cross the bridge over the River Dochart and turn right. The car park for 40 cars lies 70m along on the right. If this is full there are larger ones further on through the town, but you will have to adapt the walk.

Moirlanich Longhouse is a rare surviving example of a traditional longhouse where people lived in one end and their animals in the other. It is built with crucks and would have had a thatched roof.

In the fifteenth century the Campbells of Breadalbane bought the Auchmore lands from the MacNabs, including **Finlarig Castle**. This became their headquarters and also the place where they beheaded prisoners for whom they were unable to extract a ransom.

Moirlanich Longhouse

16

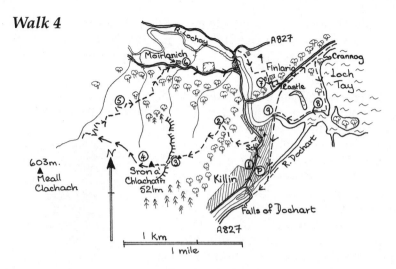

1. Return to the main road from the car park and turn right. Walk through the pleasant town to pass the primary school on the left. Shortly after this turn left through a gate into Breadalbane Park. Turn left again on the first path, which runs up the edge of the grass. At the top of the park go through the gate into the pasture beyond and continue straight ahead up the slope. Bear left at a vague Y-junction and then climb up a broad grassy swathe through the bracken-covered top of the field. Climb a ladder stile over the fence into open mature oak woodland and follow the path as it bears right to traverse the wood.

2. Near the top of the trees the path turns sharply left and then continues for a short distance just above the trees before it swings right and crosses open ground. Pass under the power line and start to climb steeply. From now on there are several steep climbs interspersed with level bits where you can get your breath back ! Eventually you arrive on a small summit with rocky outcrops and a superb view back over Loch Tay to Ben Lawers and Meall nan Tarmachan. Then go slightly downhill to cross a damp area and climb the grassy slope beyond. In summer this is colourful with lady's alpine mantle, common speedwell and tormentil.

3. Wind through a gully in low cliffs. Cross another level area and then walk up a fairly gentle slope, with an old wall on your left, until you reach a cairn at the start of the summit plateau. Continue across this to an even more substantial cairn which marks the actual

summit. Here you will want to pause again to enjoy the view. You can now see Ben More and Stobinian up Glen Dochart behind the shoulder of Meall a'Clachach, the highest point of the hill you are on.

4. Bear right as you leave the summit, heading north-west for a small rise on the edge of Glen Lochay. Cross above the start of a burn and descend the hillside a little way but do not go down onto the steeper lower slopes. There is a sloping grassy shelf below the grassy top of the hillside, with many animal tracks along it. Contour along one of these, aiming for a clump of larch trees on a cliffside ahead. The walking is easy and the grass full of heath spotted orchids in the late spring. Before reaching the trees you will notice a path coming towards you down the slope; it is more of a groove than a path and is the line of an old peat road which came up from Glen Lochay to the peat cuttings on top of the hill. Aim for this path and join it at an obvious hairpin bend, and then zigzag down the hillside on it (or beside it), checking the line if ever it becomes less obvious. In many places it has walls of stone and turf beside it and is very clear.

5. Cross a fence and go through a gap in the old stone wall, beyond. Then continue across the top of a pasture, ford a burn and wind down through another field. At the bottom go through a gate and on down the next field. The minor road up Glen Lochay comes into view and also a house with a red corrugated iron roof. This is Moirlanich Longhouse, owned by the National Trust for Scotland. Where the track curves away to the left, low down the field, turn right and follow a tractor track which heads towards the longhouse.

Melancholy thistle

Go through a gate in the electrified deer fence opposite, taking care to avoid rucksacks touching the high electric wires above the gate.

Stonechats

6. Look at the Longhouse and then turn right and walk a kilometre down the minor road to Bridge of Lochay, where there is an inn. Turn left on the main road and cross the narrow bridge, with care. A hundred metres beyond the bridge, turn right into the entrance to a golf course and walk past the clubhouse and on down a pleasing level track. There is a wall to the left with mature trees beside it. Turn left with the track, now grassy, to walk through an avenue of tall sycamores and, at the end, turn right over a small bridge, signed 'Finlarig Castle and Pier Road'. Go through the kissing gate beyond, and on down the farm track between the cottage and farm buildings to reach a road. Turn right and walk past the ruins of the castle, which stands in trees to your left. This is privately owned and in a dangerous state so you enter at your own risk, but you can walk up a path through the trees to look at the ruins from a short distance without incurring danger.

7. Return to the road and go downhill to join the pier road at the bottom and turn left. The way runs down to the old pier on Loch Tay, which was also served by a railway. Two hundred metres along, the road and the railway converge. Here go through a gap in the bushes to walk along the path on the railway, now a walkway. Ahead Loch Tay becomes visible through the trees but, before you reach it, take a kissing gate on the right to walk a path running along behind the shore. At first it is separated from the shore by a great swathe of iris. The easy way soon comes closer to the loch as it continues on a sandy embankment. There are wonderful views over the loch, to the left and, to the right, the hill you have already climbed. Look back up the loch side to see a tree-covered crannog,

its causeway made visible by rooted rushes and willows in the shallow water covering it.

8. Turn right with the path, where the river enters the loch, and go through another kissing gate to follow the river bank which, in early summer, is lined with melancholy thistles and meadowsweet. Another gate leads into a pasture, with ahead, a splendid view of Meall nan Tarmachan. Carry on until the path winds round and climbs the bank onto the old railway trackbed again.

9. Turn left and cross the bridge over the Lochay. Stroll on along the railway line. The path ends at a road in a new housing estate. Go straight ahead and where the road swings right take a path on the left to rejoin the railway track once more. Cross the River Dochart on a high bridge and swing right to walk through mature beech above the foaming water. Come down to join a track where you turn right. Walk on between two houses to come out through imposing gateposts to reach the main road. Turn right and cross the bridge, with care, below the spectacular Falls of Dochart. Turn right at the far end of the bridge and return 70m to the car park.

Practicals

Type of walk: Careful navigation required to find the path down the steep hill. Easy and delightful by Loch Tay and the rivers. Very varied walk, views superb. See information on deer stalking in Walk 3 'Practicals'.

Distance:	6–6 ½ miles/10.4km
Time:	4 hours
Maps:	OS Explorer 378, OS Landranger 51

5

Railway Trail,
Killin to Glenoglehead

Killin has several car parks. This walk starts from one at grid ref 573326. To access this, if coming from the south by the A827, cross the bridge over the River Dochart and turn right. The car park for 40 cars lies 70m along on the right. If this is full there are larger ones further on through the town.

The **Falls of Dochart** are a series of dramatic rapids that can be seen from A827 as it crosses the bridge over the River Dochart. Also, from the bridge, visitors can see to perfection the salmon run.

Falls of Dochart

By the bridge is the **burial ground of the MacNabs**. Seton Gordon in 1948 describes it:

> Through the heart of Killin the Dochart thunders, and in heavy water its spray bathes the MacNab's ancestral burial ground of Inchbuie. Inch Buie, the Yellow Island, which may have been an ancient stronghold, is densely shaded by veteran beeches and pines and golden moss covers the ground.

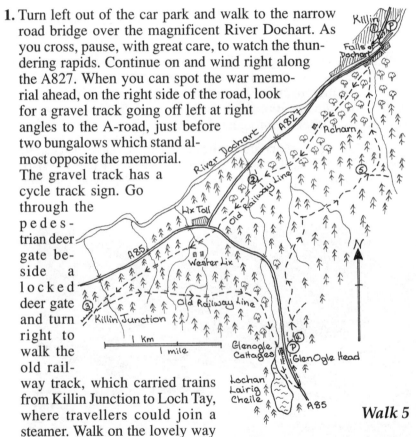

1. Turn left out of the car park and walk to the narrow road bridge over the magnificent River Dochart. As you cross, pause, with great care, to watch the thundering rapids. Continue on and wind right along the A827. When you can spot the war memorial ahead, on the right side of the road, look for a gravel track going off left at right angles to the A-road, just before two bungalows which stand almost opposite the memorial. The gravel track has a cycle track sign. Go through the pedestrian deer gate beside a locked deer gate and turn right to walk the old railway track, which carried trains from Killin Junction to Loch Tay, where travellers could join a steamer. Walk on the lovely way through deciduous woodland. Look for the pool, beyond the fence and trees on the right, where you might spot roe deer grazing the lush grass. Then the deer fencing ceases and mixed woodland stretches away on either side. Watch out for long tailed tits as you carry on the pleasing way.

Walk 5

2. On reaching a 'crossroads' of tracks, go ahead on a narrower raised track, still the old railway line. Go through a deer fence and beyond, the track opens out as you head for the A85. Cross with great care, checking that both ways are clear, and carry on up the sloping track through clear fell to rejoin the railway line. Stroll on with a sudden brief view of Glen Dochart to the west. Ignore a track coming in on your left and carry on a short distance to arrive at the old platform of Killin Junction.

Roe deer

3. After a pause in this quiet open area, walk back to the Y-junction and take the right branch, now to follow the old railway track from Oban to Callander and Stirling. This is another delightful route, from where there are fine views of the hills ahead, as the track climbs, almost imperceptibly, to the head of Glen Ogle. At an open area look left for a magnificent view of the Ben Lawers range, with shapely Meall nan Tarmachan nearest to you. Then continue on to pass Glen Ogle Cottages, which stand on the old Glen Ogle Head platform. Go on to come to the side of the A85. Cross, with care, and turn left to walk the cycle way, Sustrans Route 7, to reach a small parking area, where you might be lucky to find a mobile snack bar selling a very acceptable cuppa.

4. Go on under the overhead barrier and continue along the track. Pass through a deer gate and turn left to walk the tarmacked cycle track, downhill, passing through yellow bollards. Eventually the tarmac ends and a pleasing track, with grass down the middle, continues. Ahead is another magnificent view of the Ben Lawers range. Carry on to reach a T-junction of tracks, where you turn right. The route now makes a wide semi-circle, rising steadily, through mixed woodland where you might spot roe deer, woodpecker, jay, hen harrier and, at the right time of the year, a host of dragonflies and common blue butterflies. Soon the track levels and on the banks you might see stag's horn clubmoss.

5. At the Y-junction take the left branch and begin to descend steadily, with Killin soon coming into view. Pass through the deer gate and walk ahead to the A827. Turn right to retrace your steps to the pleasant village, where you might wish to visit the burial ground of the MacNabs, which lies to the right, through a gate in the middle of the bridge, but you have to get a key. You can walk under the bridge when the river is low.

Common blue

Practicals

Type of walk: This is a splendid walk along well-cared for tracks. As the route mainly makes use of trackbeds of old railway lines the walk seems almost level. Any climbs are very gentle.

Distance: 9 ½ miles/15.2km
Time: 4 hours
Maps: OS Explorers 378 and 365, OS Landranger 51

6

Balquhidder to Glen Dochart

This is a linear walk. It can be done by using two cars or making use of a good friend who will drop you off at the start and pick you up at the end. If neither of these options are available, retrace your steps from the pass.

Park at Balquhidder. There is space for several cars in front of the church, grid ref 536209, or there is parking space beside the village hall a short distance, west, through the village.

Today's tiny village of **Balquhidder** was once a place of some importance on an east–west running glen and a natural crossing of several hill-routes. This was formerly the country of the McLarens while the MacGregors also claimed territory here.

Go up the steps in front of the church to visit **Rob Roy's grave,** with his wife's on one side and his two sons' on the other. Behind the grave is Balquhidder's ruined kirk, which dates from 1631. It was built on the site of a pre-reformation chapel. It was once

Rob Roy's Grave, Balquhidder

(HELEN) MARY WIDOW OF ROB ROY DATE OF DEATH UNKNOWN

ROBERT MACGREGOR (ROB ROY) DIED 28 DEC. 1734 (O.S) AGED ABOUT 70

COLL DIED 1735 ROBERT DIED 1754 SONS OF ROB ROY

visited by James IV. For generations of McLarens it was their place of worship and within its walls their chiefs were buried.

William Wordsworth and his sister, Dorothy, visited the village in 1803. As they came down from Loch Voil they heard a pretty highland girl singing as she harvested. This inspired the well-known poem 'The Solitary Reaper'.

1. After visiting the famous grave and the old kirk, wind left of the new church (1853) to take a tree-lined gravelled track, directing you towards a waterfall. Beside you hurries the Kirkton Burn. Ignore the path to the right, which is your onward route, to walk to a footbridge from where you have a fine view of the delectable waterfall. Return to

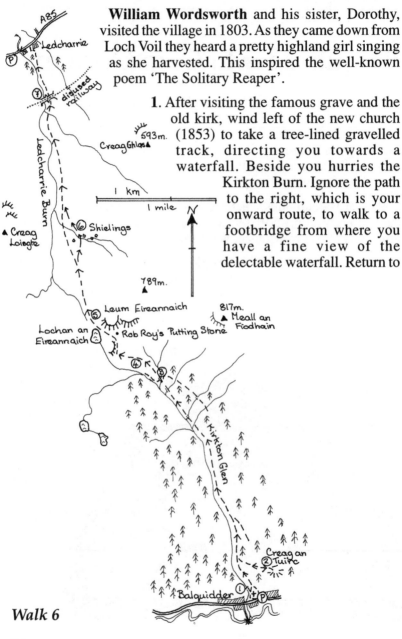

Walk 6

26

Redpolls

take the path, ignored earlier, now on your left, and signposted Creag an Tuirc and Kirkton Glen. The pleasing path climbs uphill, through trees, to go over a stile and then winds steadily through tall conifers. Watch out for the sign, on the right, directing you to Creag an Tuirc. In ½km go through a hurdle gate on the right, descend steps to cross a stream and climb up the other side. Ascend gently to a fine cairn and a seat on the top of the crag, with one of the loveliest of views below. Loch Voil stretches away, with sloping ridge after sloping ridge, dipping steeply to the water, with several summits peeping over the top. On the cairn it says 'Creag an Tuirc is an ancient rallying place for Clan McLaren'.

2. Return from the crag and on through the hurdle. Continue, left, down the path to the main track, where you turn right along the needle-lined way that leads through Kirkton Glen. Go past a track coming in on the left and then another on the right. Go ahead out into the glen to walk through clear-fell where young conifers have been planted. Stride on through a fine stand of Scots pine and walk on. As you pass through the immature conifers you might see redpolls, twites, siskins and whinchats.

3. At a junction of tracks where one winds left and the other right, look for a board signed 'Glen Dochart path'. The little path ascends

the steepish hillside immediately in front of the signboard. Climb steadily the easy-to-walk way, where stag's horn club moss thrives. The path goes up through clear-fell and tiny birches still in their protective sleeves. Carry on up through heather and bilberry to come to a fence across the slope ahead of you.

4. Turn left to cross a stream on slabs of rock and continue on the distinct path as it begins to curve right, coming close to a deer fence on your left. The path leads to a stile in the fence on your right. Beyond, go on up the distinct way past old gateposts. Then begin a rather steeper climb, keeping below crags on your left, into a shallow valley. To your right is the huge boulder, Rob Roy's putting stone. Above it is the steep craggy face of Irishman's Leap (Leum an Eireannaich). Then walk on through the lovely hollow, below the lofty crag, on a delightful green trod, to come to a fine mountain pool, the 'little loch of the Irishman' (Lochan an Eireannaich). If you can find a sheltered hollow this is the place for your picnic.

5. Then go on to pass through a gate and follow, half-right, the middle of three indistinct paths—it is the one going down beside the burn. Very soon the path becomes more substantial and a pleasure to walk as it descends gently into the wild environs of the glen of the Ledcharrie burn. If you spot the golden eagle that often frequents this high top, stop to enjoy it. And then walk on, gently descending, keeping well up the slopes above the lower boggy parts of the glen. Continue until you can see a tall cairn on a flat grassy plateau. Head left down the slope to stand by it and look around the grassy flat for several ruined shielings.

6. Look ahead from here for a series of tall posts heading down the glen (these started higher up but directed you through a much wetter area). There are considerable distances and often boggy areas between the posts. If possible choose the drier way often to be found through the bracken. This rather bleak lonely glen is shadowed by Creag Loisgte to the left and Creag Ghlas to the right. Carry on down and when you can see a post to left of a hillock with a little post on its top, wind left of the hillock along a path to go through a gate in a wall. Drift slightly left alongside another knoll and then, when you can spot a disused viaduct aim for the right arch. (If after rain the area between you and the viaduct is very boggy, wind round the hillock, right, and on reaching a great

stand of bracken, walk down beside it to the edge of a fenced woodland. Turn left and walk alongside the fence, negotiate a stream and turn right under the arch.

7. Here take a derelict stile over a fence, taking care to keep your rucksack away from the insulated wire above your head. Walk along beside the fence, on your right, for a few steps and then climb a broken stile over it, on your right (no barbs on the wire here). Descend beside the fence, cross small streams or wind round particularly mirey patches until the way becomes much drier. Carry on down a track towards Ledcharrie farm, walking with fenced woodland to your left and then past a pylon. Go through a gate into the farmyard and take another out of it and join the A85. Turn left and stroll on to the lay-by a short way along the busy road where, hopefully, the second car or your good friend will be waiting.

Stag's horn clubmoss

Practicals

Type of walk: A very satisfactory walk. A steady climb up Kirkton Glen on tracks and a clear path. The descent to Glen Dochart is not quiet so easy, with far apart posts to help you just a bit. Much wetter underfoot. See Walk 3, 'Practicals', for information on deer shooting.

Distance: 7 miles/11.4km
Time: 3–4 hours
Maps: OS Explorer 365, OS Landranger 57 and 51

7

An Sidhean from Strathyre

Park in the car park at the south end of Strathyre, grid ref 561168, where there are toilets. This lies on the west side of the A84.

Strathyre (meaning broad winding valley) is cradled by ice carved mountains. It straddles the meandering River Balvag as it flows from Loch Voil through Balquhidder, Strathyre and on to Loch Lubnaig. Once crofters grazed their cattle by the river. Now tall trees of larch, spruce and native pine, of the Queen Elizabeth Forest, cloak the hills. The village is celebrated in the traditional song 'Bonnie Strathyre' by Sir Harold Boulton. Originally the village was just a collection of cottages belonging to 'cottars', farm workers who had been cleared from the hills around Balquhidder to make way for sheep grazing. When the railway arrived in 1870 new villas and hotels were built on the west side of the river ready to welcome the stream of visitors who came, and still do, to enjoy the dramatic scenery.

River Balvag at Strathyre

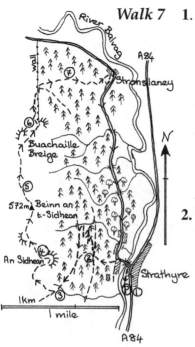

Walk 7

1. Turn left out of the car park to walk the A84 that runs through the village. As you near the end of the houses, opposite Munro Hotel, turn left down a leafy lane to cross a stone bridge over the River Balvag. Walk on up the road and at the T-junction, turn left. In a few steps take the waymarked path, going off right, to climb steeply uphill through Scots pine. Follow the path up and up to join a forest road.

2. Turn right and after 30m climb a narrow path, left, to arrive at a notice board asking you to use the new footpath. Zigzags take you 'kindly' up a very steep slope of the forest. In summer look here for fungi, very bright green moss, ferns and foxgloves. Then after more zigzags the path levels and then one more ascent brings you to another forest road. Turn left and walk on to a turning place. Here carry on along a narrow path through the trees. At a Y-junction follow the right branch, marked with blue banded posts. Stroll on the lovely needle-strewn way below lofty pines. Just beyond a waymarker, at the edge of the forest, cross a small burn on stones.

Yellow mountain saxifrage

3. Follow the distinct path as it winds right and climbs through immature spruce. Look back for a fine view of Loch Lubnaig below. Go on up through heather, bracken and bilberry as the trees are left behind. Follow the path as it begins to veer, right, and climbs more steeply. Where the path divides take the right branch and traverse the side of the hill and then on to the ridge. Here turn left and a climb a few more steps to the little

31

cairn on the knoll-like summit of An Sidhean (546m). In high summer it is covered with heather, bilberry and tormentil, all intermingled. You will want to pause here to enjoy the superb view.

4. Continue on from the cairn and drop down the steepish path with care. As you near the bottom of the knoll a path winds sharply, right, round it. Take this and after a few steps, leave it to strike left across boggy grass on a narrow path. Climb the slope beyond to a stile over a fence (you can see the stile from the summit, but it disappears from sight as you descend). Beyond the stile, climb gently past Creag Dubh on a narrow, distinct path, which passes through pink and white heather, cloudberry, bilberry and alpine lady's mantle. Then descend, always taking the main, generally wider path, when you have to make a choice. Go on down to cross a peat hag, where you will need to wind right and then left before rejoining the path, which is once more distinct. Climb steadily on the path, keeping in line with old fence posts which once marked the boundary, these acting as excellent waymarks to help you find your way up Beinn an t-Sidhean (572m).

Foxglove

5. Follow the path as it leads on to a 'stranded' gate and beyond, a fence, which you step across. Carry on along the path to descend, north, to come to an area of boggy pools. Here the path is lost. Choose the driest way across this little valley, using the fence posts to keep you on track. Very soon the path emerges and climbs, easily, up Beinn Luidh (565m). Follow the fence posts across a wide pleasant grassy flat with a huge boulder to your right. Then go up and down two hillocks where the path is not quite so easy to discern, but keep an eye open for the fence posts and keep heading north. Descend steeply down a faint path, through heather, and carry on along the path, slightly right, to come to the corner of two fences.

32

Carry on ahead, with the fence to your right, to come to a corner where the fence meets another one and there is a sturdy low wall going off left.

6. Turn left, just before the wall and continue on a path, with the wall to your right. Remain on the path for over a kilometre, keeping parallel with the companionable wall. Eventually you reach a plantation which stretches away right, beyond the wall. Carry on, gently down at first, and then you have a steep heather-clad slope to descend. There are little paths but choose the easiest way. As you drop down pause to enjoy views of Loch Voil and Balquhidder. Then the slope becomes more gentle and a faint path leads you to a gate in the friendly wall. Pass through and go on descending on the other side. After a short distance you arrive at a turning point where the forest road, beyond, makes a hairpin turn. First, jump a small burn and then join the descending road (left branch).

7. Head on down the pleasant way to join a narrow road, where you turn right. Stroll the virtually traffic-free way, passing under conifers and then through deciduous woodland, where huge beeches line the way, and moss covered walls and boulders delight the eye. When you arrive at the edge of the village, turn left and cross the bridge over the river. A few metres on, go through an iron kissing gate, on the right, to walk a wide track, below trees, behind the houses of the main street. Continue past the children's playground and then past more houses. Cross a bridge over a burn and a short way along turn sharp left to descend a gravel path. Walk ahead to pass a wooden building. The car park lies just ahead.

Practicals

Type of walk: A challenging climb through the Queen Elizabeth Forest and then more climbing over open fell and along a pleasing ridge, with a final return through more woodland. Suitable for seasoned fell walkers. Do not attempt the ridge in the mist although the old fence posts and wall are good waymarkers. Strong boots, map and compass essential.

Distance: 6 miles/10km
Time: 3–4 hours
Maps: OS Explorer 365, OS Landranger 57

8

Ben Ledi

Park before the barrier at the start of the cycle track proper, grid ref 586092. To reach this take the A84 north from Callander through Kilmahog and the Pass of Leny. Turn left, signed Strathyre Forest cabins, and cross the bridge over the river, the Garbh Uisge. Turn left and drive down the track towards the cycle track proper and park in one of the bays. If this parking area is full return to the main road and continue north for about 300m to a large lay-by on the left, grid ref 587095, and walk back to cross the bridge.

Ben Ledi, 879m, is a fine Corbett, and the highest hill in the Trossachs. It is one of the landmark hills of the Highland edge, well seen from the motorway near Stirling by people travelling north, or across the plain of Forth and Teith from the northern edge of the Campsies.

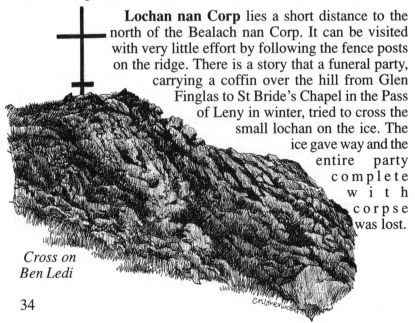

Lochan nan Corp lies a short distance to the north of the Bealach nan Corp. It can be visited with very little effort by following the fence posts on the ridge. There is a story that a funeral party, carrying a coffin over the hill from Glen Finglas to St Bride's Chapel in the Pass of Leny in winter, tried to cross the small lochan on the ice. The ice gave way and the entire party complete with corpse was lost.

Cross on Ben Ledi

1. From the end of the bridge walk north along the old railway, now a paved cycle track, towards the Strathyre Forest cabins. The river, the Garbh Uisge or Rough Water, is down to the right and you may hear oystercatchers piping. After about 1km go through a gap in the fence on the left, signed Ben Ledi, and turn right on the track beyond (i.e. go on in the same direction on a parallel track). Some 200m further on, take the left branch at a Y-junction (red waymark). At a hairpin bend in the track take a small waymarked path going right and winding through fine deciduous trees above the Stank Burn in its gorge. The burn is full of waterfalls and sounds exciting but you can't see them at this point.

1 Km

1 mile

Lochan nan Corp

Stank Glen

Loch Lubnaig

N

A84

Ben Ledi
▲ 879m

2. The path curves on up, newly repaired and fenced above the burn in exposed places. Climb up to meet a forest track at a hairpin bend, but just touch the corner before returning into tall conifers on the path. As the path turns a corner you have a good view of a waterfall at last. Continue to climb until you reach another forest track. Turn right here and then immediately left on another path, still waymarked. This is an open area which has been felled and replanted, and at the time of writing the trees are very small. The path is almost level. At the next forest track, turn right and cross the burn. Do NOT take the waymarked path which is a continuation of the one you came up on; it is very boggy and eventually dies out in a mire full of felled trees and brashings.

3. Once across the burn turn left and continue in the same direction on a forest track up the glen. The track comes to an end and a good new path continues, well drained and well aligned, marked with green footprints on posts. It crosses the burn on huge stepping stones and then winds up the hillside to the forest fence. Cross the stile and go on up the clear path until it finally reaches the ridge at the Bealach nan Corp. Here there is a line of old fence posts. (If you wish to visit the Lochan nan Corp, turn right along a path by the fence posts, about ¹/₄ to ¹/₃km north of the pass). Turn left and follow the distinct path beside them up the ridge. The walking is good; indeed as you get higher it's delightful, short grass and bilberry. Stroll along the upper part of the ridge, and now that the climbing is almost over you can enjoy the superb views. The summit has a trig point, several outcrops of rocks and a thin black metal cross erected in memory of a member of Killin Mountain Rescue who was killed on Ben More.

4. Go down the path, beyond the cross, heading towards Loch Venachar, which is spread below you. The path is like a motorway and is quite steep in places, but nothing too difficult. Cross a small intermediate summit, Meall Odhar, then descend steeply towards a wide flat shoulder with cotton grass and indistinct tyre tracks across it. Watch carefully because the path suddenly turns left here and continues as a small discreet contouring way. It winds round below the steep crags on the east side of Ben Ledi. Look here in late spring, in wet flushes, for mountain pansies, thyme, orchids and alpine lady's mantle. The path suddenly goes steeply down and is rather eroded for a short distance. Then join a revamped path and cross a stile into the top of the forest.

5. Descend steps to cross a burn and carry on down the excellent path on the lip of the ravine above the burn. Good steps made of big flat stones bring you down the steeper places. Cross a forest track and continue on the path through mature conifers. Finally wind round the hillside to emerge onto the forest track beside the bridge over the Garbh Uisge in the Pass of Leny. Turn right to return to your car.

Mountain pansies

Practicals

Type of walk: A challenging exhilarating walk. Generally well waymarked. Wonderful views

Distance:	6 miles/9.8km
Time:	3–4 hours
Maps:	OS Explorer 365, OS Landranger 57

9

Loch Venachar

Park in the Invertrossachs Estate car park, grid ref 593054, on the shore of Loch Venachar. To reach this leave Callander, south, by the A81. After a quarter of a mile and where the A-road makes a sharp left turn, take a 'no through road' that soon continues beside Eas Gobhain for nearly three miles. The parking area stands just above the road, on your left, overlooking the loch.

Loch Venachar, a reservoir, where this walk starts, is a large glorious tree-fringed, silvery stretch of water. Tracks eventually bring you above a delectable lochan, nestling among mixed coniferous woodland and not named on the map. The third loch, and the main aim of this walk, is Loch Drunkie, an idyllic pool that has curving tree-clad peninsulas that project into the tranquil water. The final pool, the Allt a' Chip Dhuibh, lies high up in the hills, the haunt of heron, goldeneye and dabchick.

High slopes mainly clad in

Loch Venachar

conifers, with areas of deciduous woodland interspersed, many heathery clearings and the four lovely sheets of water make this part of the Trossachs an area of rare beauty.

The Invertrossachs Estate is a privately owned working woodland and, although it is being managed to produce timber, the aim is also to promote other environments, including public access for quiet recreation.

Walk 9

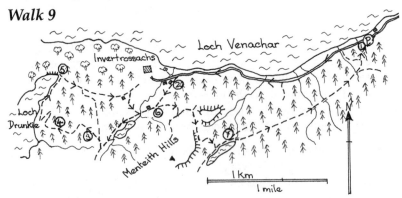

1. Turn left out of the car park and walk along the narrow metalled road, with the waters of the loch lapping the tree-clad banking to your right. To the left lie huge bushes of rhododendron, overtopped with conifers. As you go look for goldeneye bobbing on the peaceful surface of the loch. Go past the Loch Venachar sailing club. Ignore the footpath on the left and continue along the traffic-free road to pass the scouts' activity centre. Here look for the pretty waterfall opposite. At a cross of tracks, a mile and three-quarters from the car park, turn left just beyond a huge redwood tree, with a green-banded waymarker post below.

2. Pass two cottages and look ahead to see the Menteith Hills. Carry on and go left of a forest barn, Culnagreine, and head on down to cross a bridge over a burn. Here turn left to climb a wide gravelled track. Go on above the un-named lochan, which has a small dam. Here you might see more goldeneye. Soon after you have left the lochan behind you reach a right turn, which you take. A short way along, climb the banking towards the waymark on the left. Beyond this a grassy track heads up the grassy slope towards a waymarker post on the edge of a conifer plantation.

Heron

3. Once into the trees follow the waymarkers, climbing a wide ride under huge conifers. Then the track bears left and then turns sharply right. It is heavily marked with deer footprints and fox droppings. Carry on up the steepish zigzagging way, with conifers to the left and birch to the right. At the top of the ascent you come to a delectable clearing, with a picnic table close to the edge of the escarpment from where there is a superb view of Loch Drunkie.

4. Here you will want to pause before beginning your glorious descent through bell heather. Above the lovely loch the way winds right and continues as a pleasing terrace. Follow it as it descends again and then runs along the edge of a plantation. Eventually it comes close to the shore, with grand vistas across the water, the path passing through pungent bog myrtle and then a large open grassy area. Press on to the dam of the loch, where there is another picnic table.

5. Follow the path as it leaves the loch and winds right, steadily climbing through larch and birch before moving into more conifers. After half a mile you reach an open area and a waymarker post. Just before the latter, turn left onto a narrower path and begin to descend gently. It passes through mixed woodland and goes by a waymark. At the next waymark, continue down, winding left to cross a bridge over a burn and head towards a dwelling. Remain on the track until you are clear of the house and its garden, then take a good track on the right. Carry on soon to come to the bridge crossed earlier. Climb the slope to pass Culnagreine once more.

6. Three hundred metres along take the steep waymarked path, on the right, and begin your ascent through conifers and then on up a wide green track until you reach a waymarked Y-junction. Here take the right branch to continue steeply upwards through a large clearing, with conifers to your right. Very soon the path becomes stony and then climbs through a heather bank to arrive at a forest track. Turn left and in a few steps, at the T-junction, take the right turn and carry on through the Bealach nan Carn, a delightful pass through low tree-clad knolls and open heathery clearings, with higher slopes all around. Press on below a waymark, on your right, high on a heather-clad knoll and head on along the track as it curves left. Soon the Allt a' Chip Dhuibh comes into view, and then the way takes you above it. Here, look down on the charming sheet of water, where you might spot a heron waiting patiently to catch unwary prey. A small path drops down to the shore on your right and, to your left, up on a large knoll is a fine picnic table.

7. Ignore both the well signed footpath on the left and the track going right. Carry on along the wide forest track, where tall conifers eventually give way to larch and birch and there is an occasional view down to Loch Venachar. Go past two delightful burns tumbling down the steep slopes to your right and head on towards the car park. Just before it, ignore a track leading off left and wind right to return.

Practicals

Type of walk: This is a pleasing ramble on good tracks and paths. It is a good route for a windy day, the trees providing excellent shelter. The views are good and the four lochs are gem-like among the forestry. Generally well waymarked and with well-placed picnic tables.

Distance: 7 ½ miles/12km
Time: 4 hours
Maps: OS Explorer 365, OS Landranger 57

10

Brig o'Turk and Loch Finglas

Use the car park provided by the Woodland Trust on the south side of the road opposite the entrance to Lendrick Lodge, grid ref 549063. This is accessed by the A821 Aberfoyle to Callander.

Glen Finglas is the Woodland Trust's largest reserve in Scotland and lies at the heart of Scotland's first National Park, Loch Lomond and the Trossachs. It is steeped in history, at one time forming part of the royal hunting forest of Scottish kings and nobles. Originally made famous by Sir Walter Scott who mentioned Finglas Water in the 'The Lady of the Lake' and wrote about it in his epic poem 'Glenfinlas'.

Before the reservoir dam was built the **waterfalls** on the River Turk were even more spectacular than they are today. It was here that Ruskin's wife, Effie, fell in love with the painter, John Everett Millais, who had been engaged in painting Ruskin's portrait.

Loch Finglas

1. Walk out of the car park along the surfaced path beside the information board. Follow the path through oakwoods up a small valley, then uphill onto a low ridge. Turn right at the top to stroll a grassy path along the ridge. Climb the stepped way as it curves round through a kissing gate and ascends to a rock-girt summit. Here the trees come to an end and as you continue along the ridge enjoy the open views of Loch Achray and Ben Venue. Where three large boulders block the way bear right over the high ground and then descend gently, following red spots on rocks, towards the road. Walk ahead past a marked boulder, 10m to the right of an obvious path, and then cross duckboards beyond it to come down to the road at a kissing gate.

2. Cross with care and go through the gate at the far side. The path continues on duckboards round a large, very wet bog which is the remains of a curling pond. Here you might see snipe and herons, and in the summer dragonflies and damselflies. Contour round the hillside beyond on a paved path, with duckboards in wetter areas, to reach a track where you turn right. Go over a shoulder of a small hill and down a grassy path to another kissing gate. Then descend through birch woods to cross a track and come down steeply to a metalled road. Turn right.

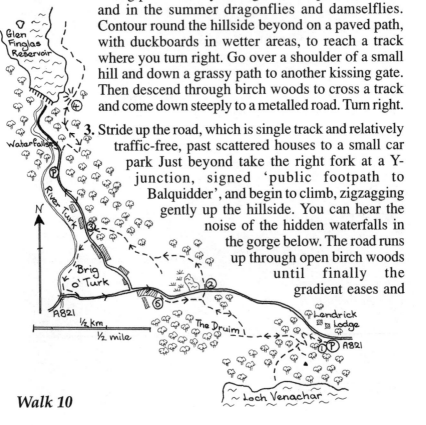

3. Stride up the road, which is single track and relatively traffic-free, past scattered houses to a small car park Just beyond take the right fork at a Y-junction, signed 'public footpath to Balquidder', and begin to climb, zigzagging gently up the hillside. You can hear the noise of the hidden waterfalls in the gorge below. The road runs up through open birch woods until finally the gradient eases and

Walk 10

42

you can see the dam far below. Ahead is a viewpoint, with a fine stone seat where you can eat your lunch whilst admiring the view of Loch Finglas and its surrounding hills. The high mountain on the right is Ben Ledi.

4. Return down the road to the car park, and turn right to go through a gate, with a board which says 'Scottish Hydroelectric, no unauthorised entry'. Turn left immediately and follow a tiny path down through the trees to the side of the River Turk. Walk upstream above the river to see the waterfalls, which must have been splendid before the dam was built; they are still well worth seeing. Take care on the slippery banks. Soon the path comes out at a passing place on the hydro road; turn right and walk back down past the car park until you reach the point at which you first joined the road. Here take a signed footpath, on the right, which follows the river bank down to the main road. Opposite the entrance to a hotel cross the road, with care, and walk along the pavement beside it, all the way through the village of Brig o'Turk. There is a teashop here, which can be recommended.

5. Beyond the last house in the village, take a path on the right, which runs parallel with the road for about 200m. Then go through a kissing gate and very soon rejoin the outward path where it went down to the duckboards. Return to the car park.

Common hawker dragonfly

Practicals

This is a very pleasant short walk, marked with red spots, mostly laid out by the Woodland Trust. Dogs may be taken on leads but not in March and April when cattle may be calving in the fields. At this time of year access may be restricted.

Distance: 4 ¼ miles/7km
Time: 2–3 hours
Maps: OS Explorer 365, OS Landranger 57

11

Ben A'an

Park in the Forestry Commission's Ben A'an car park, grid ref 509070. This is reached from the A821 between Aberfoyle and Callander, beside Loch Achray and just west of Taigh Mor Trossachs Hotel

Ben A'an (or Ben A'n) is the small conical peak on the end of the line of hills behind Loch Achray, well seen as you come over the Duke's Pass from Aberfoyle. It is quite small, only 454m high, but is very steep and rocky, with cliffs on its south face, and its position above the end of Loch Katrine means that the views from the summit are stunning. Originally it seems to have been called Am Binnein, meaning a small pointed peak, or Beannan, little mountain, but in his epic poem 'Lady of the Lake' Sir Walter Scott referred to it as Ben A'n and this has been its name ever since.

Ben A'an

1. Cross the A821, with care, and take the clear footpath, signposted Ben A'an, which leads uphill. Climb steeply along the forest edge, noting the fine example of Scots Baronial building across to the right at An Taigh Mor, and follow the well made path as it winds into the forest and continues to the edge of a deep-cut burn, the Allt Inneir; admire the fine array of wood sorrel, ferns and mosses, especially feather moss. Cross the wooden bridge over the burn and go steeply up the far bank before reaching a small level col; the knoll to the left provides a good view of Ben A'an through the trees, and back over Loch Achray.

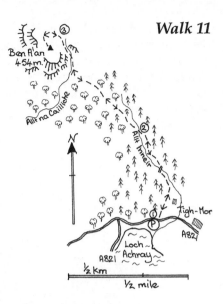

2. Stay with the path as it follows round the hill and crosses the burn on convenient stones. Then the path leads gently up out of the valley and over a flat area before reaching the edge of the trees, where another small hill provides the first clear view of Ben A'an just above, as well as affording a lovely vista over to Ben Venue. Note the good path coming steeply down the small valley to the right of Ben A'an: this is your on-going route. The path is well built and maintained, with steps for much of the next section, and winds its way up through birch scrub to meet another small burn. Watch out for the split in the path here: the best route lies on the far bank, over a clearly built crossing of stones, rather than the more obvious path up the side you are already on. After this crossing the path becomes more eroded and is very steep in places, but there are usually fairly easy ways round if you look for them. Take care on the last steep section as it is often slippery.

3. The path becomes much flatter and follows the edge of a boggy area before curving round to the left behind Ben A'an. There is another path off to the left that takes a more direct route but this is more eroded and steep. The main path has been built over the worst of the wet sections and eventually leads you over a small rise to curve left and up the back of Ben A'an's rocky summit from where there is a spectacular view over Loch Katrine and a whole array of mountains from Ben Lomond peeping over the shoulder of Ben Venue, round past the Arrochar Alps to Beinn Vorlich, and looking north, Cruach Ardrain and the twin peaks of Stob Binnein and Ben More. Remain here for as long as you like before descending by your outward route.

Woodsorrel & Feather moss

Practicals

Type of walk: This is a short but most challenging walk, with a stunning view from Ben A'an's summit. Make sure you wear boots and take waterproofs etc. with you.

Distance:	2 miles/3.4km
Time:	2–3 hours
Maps:	OS Explorer 365, OS Landranger 57

Loch Katrine

This is a two section 'walk'. The first part is delightful; travelling across Loch Katrine to Stronachlachar in the SS *Sir Walter Scott*. The second part is challenging and is done on foot over 2 ¼ miles of metalled road and then 2 ½ miles of track. This is followed by 1½ miles through boggy woodland and across wet moorland, following mostly distinct animal tracks. Then comes an almost pathless hard ¾ mile climb to the Bealach nam Bo. The next 1 ½ miles or so, takes you down the rocky pass on a path and on along a good track and minor road for the final return to the start.

SS Sir Walter Scott

Before deciding to do this walk, there are some essential considerations to be taken on board:

1. It is a summer walk; the boat, SS *Sir Walter Scott*, only plies the loch in the summer months (April to September).

2. At the time of writing, you must catch the 11 a.m. ferry because this is the only one that stops at Stronachlachar pier. Once you have disembarked, other than phoning for a taxi, there is no other way of returning except on foot. There is a postbus meets the boat but you have to be very quick to catch it.

3. Choose a reliable day, weatherwise.

4. Choose a day with long hours of daylight because of the late start.

In spite of all the above, completing this exhilarating, challenging walk will give seasoned fell walkers, who can read a map and use a compass, a great sense of achievement.

Loch Katrine was made famous by the exploits of real-life Rob Roy MacGregor. He was the man romanticised by Sir Walter Scott as his Highland hero. For hundreds of years the land about the loch was owned by the MacGregor's (children of the mist). Rob Roy, clan leader, dispossessed landowner, cattle owner and rustler, was born nearby in Glen Gyle at the head of the loch. Tradition has it that Rob Roy sought to revenge the cruel attack on his wife and the loss of his home at Craigrostan at the hands of the Duke of Montrose's men. The rent was collected by the Duke's evil factor and kinsman, Graham of Killearn. Rob Roy captured him and carried him off to the island now known as the Factor's Island (very close to where you disembark) and forced him to write to the Duke, demanding compensation for burning Craigrostan. Eventually Rob Roy let him go, unharmed; killing the factor would only have added to Rob's problems.

In 1850 a **water supply system** was developed to bring fresh water to the City of Glasgow. Large pipes divert and carry huge quantities of water from Loch Katrine to the city. A dam was built across the mouth of the loch, raising the water level and drowning some of the landmarks familiar to Sir Walter Scott and Rob Roy.

Within a few years of the publication, by Sir Walter Scott, of the poem **'Lady of the Lake',** tourists began to flock to the area. The SS *Sir Walter Scott* (smokeless fuel fired) is the last in a line of steamers to transport visitors around the loch. It was built at William Denny's boatyard at Dumbarton and carried in pieces by barge up Loch Lomond to Inversnaid. From here it was hauled up to Loch Katrine by horses and then reassembled at Stronachlachar, where bolts were replaced by rivets. It still makes daily voyages round the lake in the summer; it is a very, very quiet, glorious, popular trip.

Park at the Trossachs Pier Complex at the mouth of Loch Katrine, grid ref 496073. This lies at the western end of the A821. As the trip is very popular book your ticket as soon as you arrive at the pay-and-display car park.

Walk 12

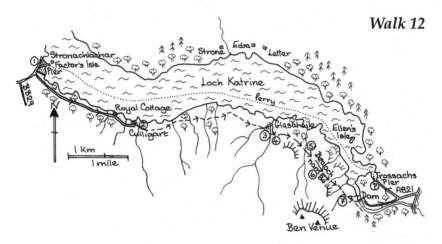

1 Leave the pier at Stronachlachar and walk along the road, to take the second turn on the left. This is a narrow almost traffic-free tarmacked road. At first it passes through fine deciduous woodland, where you might see spotted flycatchers and long tailed tits. Go on to pass Royal Cottage. Here sluices control the water leaving the loch and it is where, in 1895, Queen Victoria stayed to attend the official opening of the works. Carry on along the road to Culligart, where a gate gives access to the continuing track. On the gate, 2¼ miles from the pier, is a notice reminding you that at the end of the track the way is pathless.

2. Carry on the reinforced, rollercoaster way, for 2 ½ miles, with views ahead of Ben Venue and then Ben A'an. Ford a small burn and look ahead to see a large sheepfold and building. Here the track

ends. A few steps beyond the ford leave the track and take an indistinct grassy path, on the left. This soon comes close beside the burn you have just crossed. Then the path leads to a wider track that zigzags down to cross a tractor bridge. Go up and through a gate and bear right, through long grass, to follow the burn down stream to cross another bridge, this time a footbridge over the Allt Glasahoile. Carry on up the slope for a few steps beside the fence on your left.

Spotted flycatcher

3. Go on up a stony way, more stream than path, that veers right and then winds back left. It steadily improves and goes on as a wide grassy track, winding round the right side of a knoll. It then continues on up, parallel with the fence on your left. Carry on up to come to a tall fence post, where the fence turns left and climbs gently. Walk on up beside the fence (no path) through aromatic

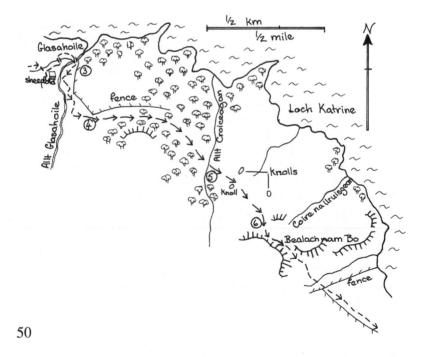

bog myrtle. Eventually you come to the next corner in the fence where there are two tall posts on either side of a hurdle gate. You are now ½ a mile from the sheepfold.

4. Go ahead on the same contour, as the fence drops down a little. Continue on deer tracks through low-growing bracken and silver birch, shadowed, on the right, by the steep tree-covered face of Creag Dhamh. Keep a look-out here for red deer. The faint path carries on, wet in places, but becomes much drier where it passes through bracken which at one point is head high. Then carry on, where the hillside to your right becomes less steep, heading slightly right, south-east, over open areas that tend to be boggy. Cross more bracken-covered gentle slopes. Look ahead to see a spur from Ben Venue with a distinct dip in it, which is the bealach you are aiming for. Then you can see a line of trees edging the Allt Chroiceagan. It is a narrow bouldery burn, which might present problems when crossing after heavy rain. Climb up the bank on the other side and look up towards the dip in the ridge and, on a nearer brow, to see two fine birches. You are now nearly ³/₄ mile from the gate in the fence.

5. Climb away from the burn, up the damp hillside, to pass to the right of two nearer birches and then head on up along the grassy edge of a large stand of bracken, on the right. Continue up to pass between two dead birches and on past the two birches you saw when you emerged from the trees about the burn. Keep going up in the same general direction picking the easiest way. Pass through scattered birch and wind round the hillock ahead. Then cross a large patch of rushes and walk on up the right side of a stream. Go on through heather and through a 'nick' in the slope.

6. Go on along a faint trod and continue past a solitary birch. Keep climbing and head for the right side of the flatter ground at the bealach. Then join a path through heather as the way climbs below the huge crags of Ben Venue. The path, now used by humans and deer, continues through the Bealach nam Bo, where legend has it, Rob Roy used to drive his cattle. You are now a hard ½ mile from the Allt Chroiceagan. Pass through the tiny gap in the large boulders ahead to begin your descent. Take your time as you go down the rocky path, with a huge boulder field to your right. When you can spot Loch Achray, with Loch Venachar to its right, stop to enjoy the pleasing view. Suddenly the distinct path gets lost in a mire but

soon emerges and is a joy to walk. Follow the path as it steadily winds round right to go through a gap in the fence and then across the hillside to come beside a burn.

7. Cross the burn on its stony bed and carry on along its right side as it turns left down to the loch. Look out for a ladderstile on the left into woodland. Once over the stile, turn right and wind round a tree-covered eminence on a little path. Descend steps to go through a gate to cross the weir, a wide railed walkway over the Achray Water. Curve right to join a metalled road. Walk on through deciduous woodland to reach the A821, where you turn left to return to the car park and the pier.

Long-tailed tits

Practicals

Type of walk: Challenging, exhilarating and often very wet underfoot. Pathless in parts.

Distance: 8 ½ miles/13.5km
Time: 5–6 hours walking
Maps: OS Explorers 364 and 365, OS Landranger 56 and 57

Inversnaid

Park in the car park, grid ref 345090, across the 'weak bridge', 100m west of the Snaid Coffee Shop. This is accessed from Aberfoyle, along the B829 to the T-junction beyond Loch Arklet, where you turn left for Inversnaid.

The waterfall at Inversnaid has inspired various writers and poets, notably Sir Walter Scott, William Wordsworth and Gerard Manley Hopkins. The latter's splendid poem 'Inversnaid' has the well known final verse beloved of conservationists:

> What would the world do, once bereft
> Of wet and of wilderness? Let them be left,
> O let them be left, wildness and wet;
> Long live the weeds and the wilderness yet.

Inversnaid is a tiny settlement at the only break in the steep slopes on the east side of Loch Lomond beyond Rowardennan. The pass above reaches only 150m by Loch Arklet. This is thought to be the result of a remnant pre-glacial drainage pattern, with a river flowing east across the present line of Loch Lomond from Glen Sloy to join the River Forth. The glacier which formed Loch Lomond cut across it at right angles, forming the short hanging valley of the Arklet Water.

Wild goat

Craigrostan, south of Inversnaid, belonged to the MacGregors from 1693, and by 1706 was all owned by Rob Roy. Many landless MacGregors settled there and pillaged their southern neighbours during the 1715 rebellion. The government afterwards annexed Rob Roy's estate and built a garrison above Inversnaid to keep the MacGregors in check. This remained until 1745, when it was seized in the uprising by the MacGregors. Little remains of it today, most of the stone having been used to build the nearby Garrison farm.

Inversnaid Falls

1. Walk uphill from the east end of the car park to visit Rob Roy's view. This is a fine vista across Loch Lomond to Ben Vane and Ben Ime. Then return to the car park. Turn left and leave the parking area by a stile in a deer fence. At a Y-junction just beyond, take the left branch and walk the level path through conifers. After about ½km the path slopes down to a kissing gate in another deer fence and then continues down into Craigrostan Woods, with crags on the left, to an old settlement called Clach Buidhe. The people who lived here used to work in the forests, cutting wood and collecting bark for tanning, but left for more lucrative jobs in the textile mills in the Blane valley and around Balfron.

2. Continue past the ruins down the old well-made path through beautiful open oak woodland, where you might in the summer spot redstarts and pied flycatchers. Go on in the direction of the loch

shore, but before you reach it curve right and climb slightly to another deer fence. Go through the kissing gate and over the low ridge. Below is the West Highland Way (WHW), and ahead through the trees you can see the Inversnaid Hotel. Descend to join the WHW and turn right on it to cross the two bridges over the Split Burn. The noise of the nearby waterfall is now loud. Turn left at the far side of the second bridge and go down steps beside the burn,

and continue right down to see the splendid waterfall which occasioned so much poetry. Then walk ahead to visit the jetty for boats from across the Loch, before walking up the ramp to the front of the hotel.

3. Cross the wide car park and take the WHW path in the far left corner. At first the path is wide and level, running along just above the shore, where you should watch out for dippers and common sandpipers. At a boathouse, go up the path beyond and then take the right turn, labelled RSPB Trail, a few metres further on. This path zigzags gently up a spur between two small burns. At the edge of the trees the path levels out and crosses a small burn on a plank bridge, then climbs to a fine viewpoint over the loch where there is a seat. You might see wild goats anywhere in these steep open woods. Beyond the viewpoint the path descends, winding down and stepped in steep places. It passes through remnants of an ancient settlement. There is another seat here, and one lower down by a large boulder. Cross a burn on a good bridge and continue steeply down to join the WHW again.

4. Turn right and follow the Way, which is considerably rougher now, though passing through delightful scenery. Go over two rocky

ridges, the haunt of wheatears, and then come to a field of enormous boulders which have fallen from the cliff a long time ago. There is a rock step across the path, which has to be climbed, but if you keep to the right side there are reasonable footholds. Beyond, the path is level between more boulders and the cliff; then descend a steep rocky staircase to a lower level. Here there is a small path off to the left, signed Rob Roy's Cave. Follow it down and round but you will have to scramble the last bit to reach the cave. Whether or not it is worth the effort is debatable because it is little more than a crack in the rock and there are several others in this group of boulders. This one is distinguished by CAVE painted in white on the right side of the enclosing rock, easily seen from the water but only from beside it on land.

5. Return to the main path to start your return. Climb back over the boulder fall. Follow the WHW past the RSPB Trail and back to the boathouse and then the hotel. Cross the bridge above the waterfall and take the left branch, signed Rob Roy View and car park, at the Y-junction beyond, then another left branch very shortly afterwards. Climb steeply uphill to a deer fence then along to a viewpoint, with a seat, looking over another fine waterfall. The stepped path continues to climb and zigzag up the steep side of the gorge. Please do not cut the corners because this leads to erosion of the carefully built path and will make it unusable. At the top of the bank the path levels out and goes through a deer fence by a kissing gate and into an open grassy area. There is a seat here too. At the next kissing gate in a deer fence go into a plantation and follow the level path to its junction with your outward route. Climb the stile back into the car park.

Practicals

Type of walk: A lovely walk all on paths. Dogs are allowed on leads as far as Inversnaid but not at all in the RSPB reserve. The WHW is quite tricky above Rob Roy's cave and to get into the cave requires a scramble.

Distance: 4 miles/6.5km
Time: 2–3 hours
Maps: OS Explorer 364, OS Landranger 56

Loch Chon

Park in the first car park beside Loch Chon, grid ref 428043, which is shown as 'boathouse' on the OS Explorer map. If this is full there is a forestry commission car park 300m further north. To reach the parking areas take the B829 from Aberfoyle to Stronachlachar.

Loch Chon is a relatively large natural lake lying at an altitude of 100m. It drains south to Loch Ard and thence to the Forth Valley. It is surrounded with forestry plantations but the woodlands round the loch are still largely of native deciduous trees.

At the time of building the **Loch Katrine aqueduct** there was a camp for the navvies beside Loch Chon. They lived in turf-roofed huts. Some navvy camps had schools, shops and churches. The one at the head of Loch Chon was nicknamed 'Sebastopol' after the famous battle of the Crimean War, due to the incessant blasting operations that were required to complete a tunnel.

Air shaft

1. Before you set off on this walk, admire the white and yellow water-lilies in the loch by the car park. Then return to the road and turn right. Walk past the small reed-fringed lochan, Loch Dhu, and turn right onto a clear track signposted 'Rowardennan'. Cross the bridge over the outflow from Loch Dhu and then walk round the back of Loch Dhu Cottage and Loch Dhu House. At the T-junction, turn right and follow the track down to the shore of Loch Chon. Enjoy the fine view across the hills to the north of the loch and the wooded islands of the birch- and alder-fringed loch. Look for buzzards overhead and for common sandpipers around the shore as you go.

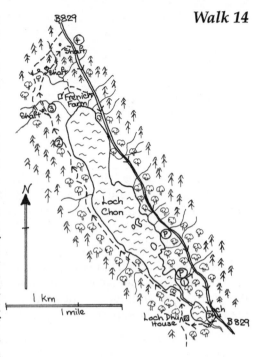

2. Eventually the way leaves the edge of the loch and passes through conifer plantations, with silver fir to the left. Then the route continues through a more open area with the aqueduct from Loch Katrine seen among the trees on the left. Soon the buildings of Frenich farm appear below on the right, and the track carries on towards a burn. At this point there is an air shaft for the aqueduct to the right of the track; it is a splendid structure with a latticework iron dome over the top.

3. Here take a pleasing grassy path that runs down from the track

Common sandpiper

58

and passes to the right of the air shaft. Cross a burn on a footbridge, where a pretty waterfall descends below. Climb the far bank through mature oak woodland, ignoring a path on the right which leads to a small stone building, an access to the pipeline. Go through a wooden gate in a wire fence, then a gate gap in an old wall. Cross the hillside on a grassy path through bracken, with wooden or metal bridges over all the burns and ditches. At the next air shaft join a pleasing mossy track, which winds round to the right and soon ends at the road.

4. Turn right to walk the fairly quiet road. Conifers slope up the hills to your left but the road runs through a wide band of deciduous trees, beside the loch. Walk past the forestry commission car park and continue for 300m to the boathouse car park.

White waterlily

Practicals

Type of walk: A very easy mainly level ramble. The return is along a fairly quiet road, but beware of tourist buses on their way to Stronachlachar and Inversnaid.

Distance: 6 ½ miles/10.5km
Time: 3–4 hours
Maps: OS Explorers 364 and 365, OS Landranger 56

15

Ben Venue

Park in a large lay-by by Loch Ard opposite the track to Ledard farm, grid ref 459023 for the ascent from the loch. Or park in a lay-by beside the A821 just south of the entrance to the Loch Achray Hotel, grid ref 505063, if starting or being picked up here. There are three lay-bys, so parking should not be a problem. Access the area by the B829 from Aberfoyle to Kinlochard, and the A821 to Loch Achray.

This walk is written assuming the use of **two cars**, or a friend to drop you and pick you up again. If this is not possible, start and return by the route from Kinlochard.

Ben Venue is a fine rugged peak, with two summits, the higher 729m and the other 727m. It is very steep and craggy and stands above Loch Katrine. Its name probably means 'small mountain'

Pool on the Ledard Burn

from the Gaelic Beinn Mheanbh; this name may seem unfair but looking at the mountains of the Trossachs from near Stirling it is indeed a small one.

The **waterfalls** on the Ledard Burn were much admired by Sir Walter Scott and he described them in two novels, *Waverley* and *Rob Roy*.

Walk 15

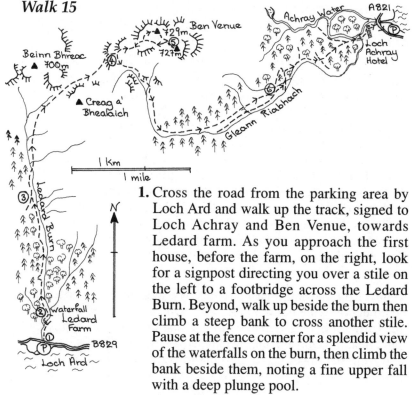

1. Cross the road from the parking area by Loch Ard and walk up the track, signed to Loch Achray and Ben Venue, towards Ledard farm. As you approach the first house, before the farm, on the right, look for a signpost directing you over a stile on the left to a footbridge across the Ledard Burn. Beyond, walk up beside the burn then climb a steep bank to cross another stile. Pause at the fence corner for a splendid view of the waterfalls on the burn, then climb the bank beside them, noting a fine upper fall with a deep plunge pool.

2. Continue along the path as it levels above the falls and runs through a delightful oakwood. Then follow the path as it ascends again. Cross a stile into a plantation and then, after a very short distance, turn right to cross another stile out of the trees. Now you are high above the burn, which is deep in its ravine. Carry on along the shelf-like path through birch woodland. At an indistinct Y-junction take the higher path.

3. Finally leave the birches and turn right on a wider track. Cross the

burn on convenient stones and climb the stile over a deer fence to carry on up the glen. Press on along the path as it swings round to follow the glen as it winds to the right. There are some peaty, boggy areas here and you should pick the driest way. Pass through a cleft at the head of the glen, with Beinn Bhreac to your left and Creag a'Bhealaich to your right, both fine craggy slopes. Suddenly you can see Loch Katrine below. Cross a stile and follow the path as it contours the open hillside. Go on climbing steeply over a rocky hummock and then down to a col. There is a large cairn here and a path off to the right, which you should note for your return.

4. Go straight ahead to climb the path at the far side of the col; it is very steep and quite eroded but there is a zigzag path at the right, which makes the ascent easier. Then the gradient eases and you have to pick your way over wet peat. Then comes another steep climb followed by another level area. At the far side of the next hillock the path descends and divides; take the left branch which ascends very steeply (with some easy rocky bits) to the north-west top of Ben Venue, at 729m the actual summit. (The right branch at the division of the way, avoids the summit and climbs directly to a col between the two tops). From the col there is a final stiff pull-up to the south-eastern summit (727m) with its trig point, where you are rewarded for all your effort with a splendid view across Loch Katrine to the north and along Lochs Achray and Vennachar to the east.

5. Return from the south-east summit by using the bypass path, and go on down to the col with the cairn, which you noted on the way up. Turn left here to descend along a distinct but very boggy path into Gleann Riabhach, taking care as you descend the steep tricky step from the upper corrie into the lower part. After this the path

Wheatear

62

improves. Soon you reach the trees of Achray Forest. Cross a stile into the plantation and follow the excellent new path on down, with blue waymarkers to help walkers on their way up! Follow the path as it leaves the plantation and goes on across a felled area and then on down to a forest track, which you cross.

6. Walk on down the continuing path to go over a small burn to another forest track, where you turn left for about 200m before turning, right, down another newly made section of the path. This passes through a very pleasant open area with scattered trees to a turning circle. Do not take the obvious new path going left but carry on down the old track, with the burn to your right. Go straight over a cross of tracks, then turn right at the next junction, above the Achray Water. This pleasant old track comes out round the back of the Achray Hotel; go left round the main building and out down the drive to the main road. Turn right to return to the parking lay-by.

Golden eagle

Practicals

Type of walk: Challenging; suitable for experienced fell walkers. Ben Venue is a fine hill with a relatively straightforward ascent and descent, but with a craggy complex summit ridge, easy enough in good weather but could be tricky in bad conditions. Boots and warm clothing should be worn. Take a map and compass. Dogs are permitted but keep them on leads through the farm.

Distance: 7 ½ miles/12km
Time: 5–6 hours
Maps: OS Explorer 365, OS Landranger 57

16

Loch Ard and Duchray Water

Park in the well signposted large car park in the centre of Aberfoyle, grid ref 521009.

Aberfoyle, sometimes named the enchanted village, rests on the banks of the River Forth, beneath the imposing cliffs of Craigmore, meaning the big crag. It is the western gateway to the Trossachs and is an area rich in folklore and tradition. It is often called the fairy capital of Scotland and is the setting for stories both fictional and real and of fairy folk and heroes like Rob Roy MacGregor who was born nearby.

Aqueduct, Loch Ard forest

1. Turn left out of the car park and, using the pavement on the right side of the road, walk along the A821 to the crossroads. Continue ahead along the B829 in the direction of Milton for just over a mile. This is a pleasant walk along a quiet road, with the River

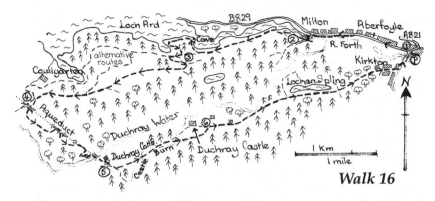

Walk 16

Forth winding charmingly through alders on the left, and with the sheltering hill, Craigmore, lined with birches, to your right. When the pavement ends, cross and continue on a footpath on the other side of the road. Soon it drops below the road and close beside the hurrying river, where you might spot a dipper. At the Y-junction take the left fork, cross the river and continue past the old mill at Milton. Where the road ceases to be metalled and you have passed the last house, turn right through a parking area (forestry commission) to stroll a pleasing rising track which passes through woodland, with branches laden with lichen.

2. Follow the gated forest track for a mile-and-a-half as it winds left and carries on the charming way beside the foot of reed-fringed Loch Ard. Ignore a left turn and continue on following the red-banded waymarkers. Then the loch widens and you have wonderful views to the hills. On the water you might spot goldeneye, merganser, pochard and dabchick. At the next right turn you may wish to make a delightful diversion to walk round a promontory. The good path passes through deciduous woodland and comes close to the shore and, sometimes, high above. Look over the railed section where you can imagine Rob Roy emerging from one of his many caves. Follow the path as it winds round the edge of the promontory. Just before it rejoins the forest track, take the path off left to a railed platform from where you have a good view of an old settlement.

3. After rejoining the main track walk right, for less than a quarter-of-a-mile, just above a delectable bay. Beyond, take a sharp left turn (red waymarker) to climb a track that passes through conifers. Follow this to the brow (¹/₄ mile) and then bear right. Where the

track soon curves left, go ahead on a continuing track (signed with a cyclists' red waymarker) parallel with the shore of the loch but high above it. Enjoy the fine glimpses of the loch and the surrounding hills. Carry on this track, ignoring both a left turn and then a right turn, for a mile-and-three-quarters to arrive at a junction of paths.

4. Turn left with, ahead, a dramatic view of the aqueduct, carrying water from Loch Katrine, with more mountains beyond. Then immediately take the left branch off the main track to pass under the left end of the aqueduct. Follow the grand track, grassed down the middle, as it winds left remaining parallel with the water pipeline. Pass an inspection chamber where you can see the water surging along. Go on the delectable way to pass under another aqueduct and then weave back under it again and stroll on. Pass the valve house, high on its slope, and then walk beside a wall and over the pipeline deep in its raised bank. Beyond descend the huge curves in the track and cross the stiled Duchray Bridge over the wildly-flowing Duchray Water, with the huge pipeline, that has descended straight down the hill-slope, beside you. Notice the way the banks of the river are being cleared of conifers to improve the quality of the water.

5. Carry on past Duchray cottages and, a mile from the first aqueduct, bear left, off the main track, walking a wide curve. Here begin your one-and-a-quarter mile gradual descent on a wide forest track, with the Castle Burn first on one side and then on the other. Here you might spot long-tailed tits in the birches that edge the hurrying water. Ignore the indistinct track to Duchray Castle and curve right to ascend a little. Ignore the next right turn and go on following the 'yellow' cycle track waymark to arrive at a junction.

Pochard

6. Here bear right, away from the access track to Duchray House and walk on along the valley bottom to pass two cottages. Remain on the main track, ignoring a right turn and continue where Duchray Water is now well below you, on your left. As pretty Lochan Spling comes into view do not take the left turn but carry on beside the peaceful stretch of water which pleasingly reflects the hillside above. At the foot of the lochan, keep ahead on the main track, which descends steadily through oak and birch woods, and then between houses to join a road. Look ahead to see Doon Hill, with its oaks and pine, and then turn left and cross the narrow bridge over the River Forth. Beyond turn right to return to the car park.

Redstart

Practicals

Type of walk: A long ramble that starts with some road walking, on pavement, and then continues on good forest tracks. Fine views for much of the way. Take time to admire the architecture of the aqueducts.

Distance: 11 miles/17km
Time: 5–6 hours
Maps: OS Explorer 365, OS Landranger 57

***NB** The walk takes you through a 'working' forest. Be prepared to adapt your route if at any time your progress is stopped because of felling etc. Use the map to work out an alternative route.*

17

Highland Boundary Fault Trail

Park at the Visitor Centre above Aberfoyle, grid ref 518014. To reach this take the well signed A821, north, from the west end of Aberfoyle's main street. Climb the twisting road, the Duke's Pass, to the parking area that lies on your right.

This walk combines the Waterfall Trail and the Highland Boundary Fault Trail in the **Queen Elizabeth Forest Park** (QEFP). Both trails have interesting information boards at appropriate places on the walk. The QEFP was first designated as a forest park by the forestry commission in 1953 to mark the coronation of Queen Elizabeth II. The park encompasses the land from the east shore of Loch Lomond to the rugged terrain of Strathyre and includes mountain and moorland, forest and woodland, rivers and lochs. It is home to a rich variety of animal and plant life.

Perched high above Aberfoyle, on the very edge of the Highlands, stands the **David Marshall Lodge (QEFP visitor centre)**. The magnificent building, with its spectacular views, was gifted to the forestry commission in 1960 by the Carnegie Trust under the chairmanship of David Marshall.

Waterfall of the Little Fawn

68

Walk 17

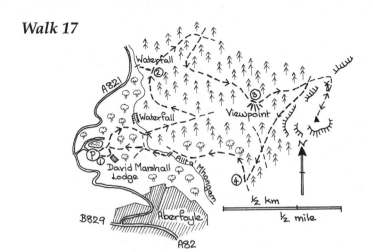

1. From the car park walk towards the left side of the visitor centre. Descend railed steps and then the railed blue trail to reach a grassy triangle. Go ahead to cross a long boardwalk, which protects the plants of the bog below. Turn right and continue through birches, soon to wind on down through more trees to come to the side of the burn, the Allt a'Mhangam. Look up stream to see the superb fall, named by the forestry commission, the Waterfall of the Little Fawn. Continue on the railed way to cross a footbridge over the brawling burn. Beyond, join a forest track and climb left through larch, still on the blue trail. Follow it where it swings sharp left and continues to climb.

2. Just after the next waymark take a narrow path, on the left, to descend a little beside a narrow stream to see another superb waterfall on the burn, tumbling in great haste down its rocky tree-lined bed. Return to the forest track and go on, left, uphill to come to a cross of tracks, where you bear right. Pause by the cliff face of Leny Grit, which is metamorphosed sand and gravel, and then carry on along a delightful shelf-like path. You soon reach a picnic table from where you have a dramatic view over Aberfoyle and the surrounding countryside.

3. Press on uphill to pass the Highland Boundary Fault line. Then carry on until you reach the tree-line and here you have a choice, either to turn right to descend or, to go on, steeply uphill, on a clear

narrow path to a fence. Once through the gap in the fence bear right on a track to reach a wonderful viewpoint on a hillock of the Menteith Hills. From here you need return to the tree-line. Whatever your choice then descend the steepish way with conifers to your right, where you might spot siskins hanging upside down on the branches, hunting for insects. This path uses the bed of an old inclined railway that once transported limestone from the Lime Craig quarry above down to kilns at Aberfoyle to be turned into quicklime. As you descend look right, across the intervening forest, to see the visitor centre perched on its hill, with Craigmore beyond. Continue steeply downhill. Then cross a track to descend another steep path down the hillside to join a lower forest road.

4. Turn right and walk the pleasing way through the mixed woodland. Watch out for the left turn signposted 'visitor centre'. Cross a footbridge and climb the slope beyond. Bear right and at the signpost ignore both its 'arms' and go straight ahead to take the rising railed way towards the centre. Continue on up if you wish to enjoy a cuppa or turn right and then left to return to the car park.

Siskin

Practicals

Type of walk: Very much an 'all way up and then all way down walk'. It takes you past two lovely waterfalls, climbs above the tree-line and leads you along some very pleasant forest tracks.

Distance: 4 miles/ 6.5km Add on half a mile if you decide to visit the viewpoint
Time: 2–3 hours
Maps: OS Explorer 365, OS Landranger 57

Inchmahome Priory

Park in the car park, grid ref 583010, adjacent to the jetty for the boat trip to Inchmahome Priory, at Port of Menteith. This lies at the north end of the B8034. It is accessed from the A81, east of Aberfoyle.

The priory ruins lie on the largest of the three islands, **Inchmahome,** on the Lake of Menteith. The island is approached, during the summer, by a motor boat from the jetty at Port of Menteith. Pay for your ticket at the shop on the island, where there are toilets nearby. If the boats are all moored at the island's jetty attract attention by the white disc found on the mainland jetty.

Inchmahome Priory

In 1547, on the outskirts of Edinburgh, the English defeated the Scots. Worried about the safety of Mary, the four-year old **Queen of Scots**, her mother, dowager Queen Marie of Guise, brought her from Stirling Castle to Inchmahome. Here they received sanctuary, and protection from the infant's guardian, the son of Lord Erskine.

Water from higher ground drains into the shallow, freshwater **Lake of Menteith**. It is a tranquil, reed-fringed pool, where water lilies grow, with a dramatic backdrop of the Menteith Hills. It is much enjoyed by anglers, and ospreys, too, and is surrounded by private pastures. Once it was known as Loch of Inchmahome but, as the beautiful priory ruins attracted more and more Victorian tourists from England, they influenced the change of name. In very cold winters the lake freezes and turns into a marvellous ice rink. It then attracts hundreds of curlers.

The Earl of Menteith, who founded the priory, lived on Inch Talla, the second largest island. The smallest, Dog Isle, is believed to be where the earl's dogs were kept or it might be named after Thomas Dog, who was prior of Inchmahome in the late fifteenth century.

Walk 18a

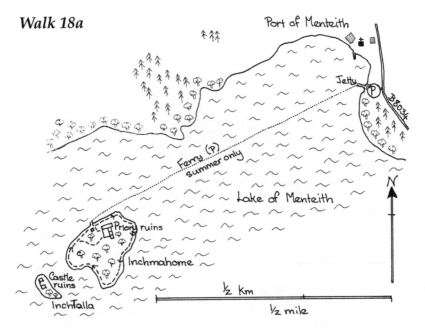

Osprey

From the jetty, walk ahead towards the little shop, where you might wish to purchase a guide to the romantic ruins. Wander at will around the priory site and soak up the magical atmosphere. Then set off, clockwise, along a distinct path near to the loch shore, through the fine woodland. As you go enjoy the ancient trees, including one with fascinating exposed roots and another, a huge chestnut tree with a split trunk. Make a short detour to see Queen Mary's garden. Stroll on the delightful way, with the water of the lake lapping beside you. Carry on past huge oak trees and ponder on all the tales these trees could tell. Continue along the western shore, looking over towards Inch Talla, to return to the jetty.

Practicals

Type of Walk: A tiny walk but a lovely interlude that should not be missed.

Distance:	¹/₄ mile/0.5km
Time:	¹/₂–2 hours
Maps:	OS Explorer 365, OS Landranger 57

18b

Doon Hill and Fairy Knowe

Park at Lemahamish, grid ref 529992, south of Aberfoyle. To reach this, leave Aberfoyle by the A821 in a south-east direction. Then join the A81, close to the Rob Roy Hotel, going south, and continue to take the first right turn for Gartmore. Cross the bridge over the River Forth and climb half way up the hill beyond, to take the first, and unsigned, rough (in parts) track, going off right into the forest. Go right at the next two junctions to come to the small parking area, under pines and close to a wide stretch of the River Forth.

The Reverend Robert Kirk was minister of Aberfoyle from 1685 to his death in 1692. Legend has it that fairies carried him off because he took too keen an interest in their affairs. In spite of being a man of the cloth fairies fascinated him. In 1691 he published, *The Secret Commonwealth of Elves, Fauns and Fairies*, an account of the lives of fairies and

Path, Doon Hill

other spirits. A year later he died while taking his daily stroll on Doon Hill. Tradition has it that he was spirited away to the underworld by the angry fairies whose secrets he had revealed. A changeling or human form was left in his place and it was buried in the minster's plot in the graveyard. Soon after the funeral the Reverend Kirk appeared in a dream to his cousin and asked that a knife be thrown at his apparition when he appeared at the cousin's child's christening. The cousin was so overcome by the minister's appearance that he didn't throw the knife and it has been said ever since that the minister's spirit is trapped forever in the pine tree that stands amid oak on the top of Doon Hill.

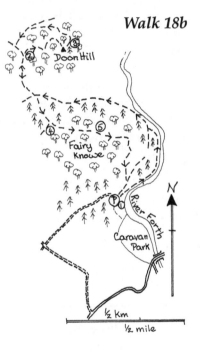

Walk 18b

1. From the parking area, take a short, narrow path to come to the side of the river. Turn left and walk on through conifers, with the Forth to your right, to join the forest road in ½km and walk right. At the cross of tracks, wind right. Just past a turning circle take, on the right, a waymarked path, signed Doon Hill, ½ mile.

2. Climb, steadily, a reinforced path, through mature oaks, which soon becomes stepped and quite steep. Carry on along a well surfaced terrace-like path before beginning another steepish climb. One more turn and you reach the crown of Doon Hill, with the famous pine looking just slightly 'weary' among the thriving oaks. At the time of writing, it was draped with ribbons on which wishes were written. There were many more ribbons suspended from the surrounding bushes and low branches of oaks. The fairy atmosphere was slightly lost and the minister's spirit failed to communicate but the sunlight sloping through the trees was delightful.

3. Return across the crown of the hill and go past your upward route and, almost immediately, take the next left turn. Descend a good

75

path through the oaks and follow it as it winds steadily, making a much more gentle descent, left, to arrive at a track. Turn left and join the forest road, where you turn left again. Climb a small slope and go past the signposted path taken earlier and carry on to the cross of tracks. Here, ignore the track right, and the one left, and climb the middle one, which carries on and up, straight ahead.

4. Where the track swings right, go ahead on a narrow grassy trod. In July you might spot ringlet moths crowding the vegetation. Follow the path as it passes through irises and then go on under rowan, ash birch, hazel and oak hung with honeysuckle. As you progress the path is reinforced in parts and there are natural sandstone slabs to cross. To the left is an ancient hazel hedge and to your right coppiced hazels. Stroll on into an open area, with a lovely view across to the Menteith Hills on your left, and the highest part of Fairy Knowe to your right.

5. Then begin your gentle descent, through the fine woodland, on the winding path. Eventually the way winds right through another open area, full of bracken and completely surrounded by trees. Follow the good path as it curves left and then right again to join a forest road. Turn right to take a few steps back to the parking area.

Ringlet

Practicals

Type of walk: A very pleasing short walk, on paths, tracks and forest roads, with several little climbs to the top of two tree-clad hills. This walk is just right for an evening stroll in summer or a brisk walk on a winter's day.

Distance: 3 miles/5km
Time: 1–2 hours
Maps: OS Explorer 365, OS Landranger 57

19

Ben Lomond

Use the large car park at Rowardennan at the end of the road, grid ref 360987, where there are toilets and a visitor information point. To reach this use the B837 from Drymen, which becomes unclassified beyond Balmaha. Drymen is reached from Glasgow by the A809.

Ben Lomond, the beacon hill, is the most southerly Munro, and stands in an isolated position on the edge of the Highlands, dominating the view on the east side of Loch Lomond. It is Glasgow's own mountain and therefore very popular; the tourist route by which this walk descends can be very busy especially at weekends and holidays. The Ptarmigan route is much quieter.

The **Ben Lomond National Memorial Park** was created in memory of all the Scots who died in military service during the 1939–45 war. It was formally opened in 1997, on Remembrance Day, and the monument on the loch shore at Rowardennan commemorates this. The area is administered by the National Trust for Scotland (NTS). In fact Ben Lomond enjoys the dubious distinction of having been bought twice with public funds 'for the Nation'. The first time it was given to the forestry commission to

Ben Lomond across Loch Lomond

administer. They planted regular blocks of non-native conifers, which was not very popular and then in 1982 declared their intention of selling off all the high land into private ownership. An outcry followed; the Countryside Commission for Scotland put up the full purchase price and the land was handed over to the National Trust.

1. Walk north from the car park to the sculpture on the shore of Loch Lomond, and then continue along the shore following the West Highland Way (WHW) signs. Take the right fork at a Y-junction and beyond a gate go on through pleasant deciduous woodland, where oak predominates. Ignore the track to Ardess and press on to cross a bridge over a burn. Carry on past the NTS Ranger Centre and then a white cottage to cross another burn. On the far side take the small path on the right which leaves the WHW and goes up through open mossy oak woodland beside a small waterfall. Pass through a kissing gate and climb uphill through scattered mature trees, where you

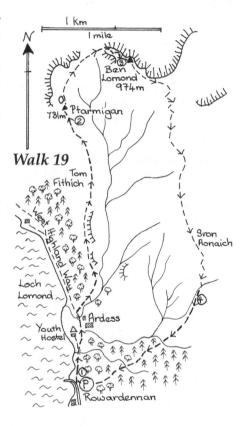

might spot long-tailed tits in the trees, and in the autumn and winter you might see flocks of redwings and fieldfares. By an old sheepfold go through another kissing gate and follow the well made path which zigzags steeply uphill with the burn to your right. High up the hill the path heads away from the burn, now a series of waterfalls in a ravine, to cross the hillside below a line of broken crags and then curves up towards a ridge. Cross another fence and

78

Redwings eating hawthorn berries

carry on up the ridge, Tom Fithich, from where there are splendid views down to your left over Loch Lomond and across to Beinn Vorlich and the Arrochar Alps. The top of Ben Lomond is across a shallow valley on your right

2. The ridge narrows to the subsidiary top called Ptarmigan, which is rocky and hummocky and has pools where you can paddle on a hot day! Descend a little beyond this top to a bealach, then begin the steep pull up to the summit of Ben Lomond. There is a good path but it is quite scrambly in places and you may need to use your hands. However it is not difficult in normal conditions and the summit is soon reached. There is a magnificent view to the north, and the shape of Ben Lomond itself becomes apparent; instead of a great dome, which is how it appears from Loch Lomond, the top is a narrow ridge, cut away on the north-east by a substantial corrie where snow may linger late into the spring. There is still plenty of space to sit on the flat slabs of rock and enjoy your well earned lunch.

3. Leave this eyrie, south-east, along the clear path on the ridge. In half a kilometre veer away from the edge of Coire a'Bhathaich and go south down a steep spur. This is followed by a long gradual descent for about 2 ½ km along the top of a broad spur called Sron Aonaich. The path has been seriously restored and gives good walking.

4. Eventually the path curves round to the south-west and comes down through a kissing gate in a fence and then on to the top of the forest. Cross the Ardess Burn and go through another kissing gate, then follow the steep path down the forest ride. Finally the gradient eases and the conifers give way to more open oak woodland. Continue through the trees to the car park.

Heath spotted orchid

Practicals

Type of walk: This is a steep exciting climb, combined with some fine ridge walking from where there are magnificent views. The paths are good. Be prepared for an energetic day because the start is not much above sea-level. All the usual cautions about climbing Munros apply.

Distance: 7 miles/11.4km
Time: 6–7 hours
Maps: OS Explorer 364, OS Landranger 56

20

Sallochy

Park in the Sallochy parking area on the shore of Loch Lomond, grid ref 380958. This is reached by the B837 from Drymen, passing through Balmaha and on beyond Cashel and the settlement of Sallochy itself.

The **Sallochy oaks** were felled by the men and the women and children stripped the bark and stacked it to dry. The felled timber was used to smelt iron in bloomeries on the shore of the loch. The oak bark was used by the leather tanning industry.

The West Highland Way (WHW) was the first long distance footpath to be established in Scotland. It runs for 95 miles/ 152km from Milngavie northwards to Fort William. It follows ancient and historic pathways and makes use of old footpaths of the Highlanders and the drove roads by which they herded their cattle southwards to the markets. It also traverses old military roads built mainly by troops to help catch the Jacobites. It uses farm roads, old coaching roads and beds of disused railways.

Loch Lomond

Walk 20

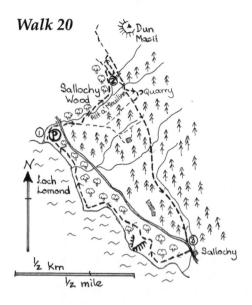

1. Walk back from the shore towards the minor road and take the few yards of the signed path, on the right, to cut off a corner to come to the roadside. Cross and walk up the narrow path opposite, which climbs gently through a wide ride in the forest, with conifers to the right and larch set back to the left. Where the path divides take the unsigned left branch to walk beside a pretty tumbling burn, passing through the oaks of this most attractive glen. After passing a blue waymarker, cross a footbridge to the other side of the dancing stream and walk on. At the next waymark, turn left up a slope, on the left, to reach a deer fence adorned in orange netting to alert and protect game birds from flying into it. Walk right, with the fence to your left and beautiful oak woodland to your right. Follow the blue waymarked path as it winds right into the trees. Go up a slope and wind round right to descend a ride to the next waymark.

2. Turn left and climb a steepish gravel and grassy path through more pleasing woodland then open ground to join a wide forest road. Look ahead and slightly left to see a shapely conical hill, Dun Maoil. Turn right and descend for nearly a quarter-of-a mile. Just after a blue waymark, take a narrow path, left, to walk a short diversion. This leads through an idyllic part of the oak woodland to pass between an old small slate quarry on the left and two heaps of spoil on the right, with an interesting information board close

Pied wagtail

by. The path then continues, leading you through the woodland to rejoin the forest road. Turn left and descend to the road.

3. Descend left for 100m to cross and take the WHW that leads off right and heads through oaks towards the shore of the loch, where wagtails flit from rock to rock. Follow the delightful path as it takes you through more glorious oaks. Then after this very pleasing stretch the path turns inland and climbs upwards, first by a path and then by steps beside a huge rock face to a ridge above. Where the trees are not too dense you should, with care, have a fine view up the loch. Having crossed over the large crag go on down a gravel path, which descends easily almost to the road. The path then swings towards the shore once more and eventually leads you out on to the beach at the Sallochy parking area.

Practicals

Type of walk: A pleasing walk through oak woodland and along the shore of Loch Lomond.

Distance:	2 ½ miles/4km
Time:	2 hours
Maps:	OS Landranger 56, OS Explorer 364

21

Cashel

Park beside Cashel within 'the forest for a thousand years', grid ref 399941. To reach this take the B837 from Drymen and drive on along this minor 'no through road' for 6 miles.

The aim of **Cashel** is to demonstrate the restoration and regeneration of Scotland's native woods through sound forestry practice. The woodland walks have been designed especially for walkers. Well graded climbs enable you to enjoy the stunning views from the higher paths. Walkers are asked to keep to the footpaths for their own safety and to avoid disturbing the abundant wildlife as little as possible. Cashel is open for walking 52 weeks of the year.

If you manage to visit Cashel when the paths are dusted with snow you will enjoy trying to identify the many **prints left by the animals and birds** that have used the footpaths too. Look for the

Cashel entrance

trail of a fox, with each print turning away slightly from the one following and with two clawed toepads pointing forward and with two clawed toe pads behind. Keep a

Black grouse

look out for the circular prints of an otter. You sometimes can see web between the toes. Rabbit prints are easy to spot with one print behind the other and then two together. These are prints of back paws, placed beside each other and sometimes slightly in front of the forepaws. The prints are blurred by fur between the toes. Wood mice and voles often trail their tails behind their prints made by their tiny four-toed clawed front feet and five-toed clawed back feet. Red deer show two pointed oval hoof marks, facing in on each other and, similarly, but half the size, are those of the roe deer. Watch out for the very definite three-toed print of the many red grouse and also the much larger, but similar print, of the black grouse often with wing prints.

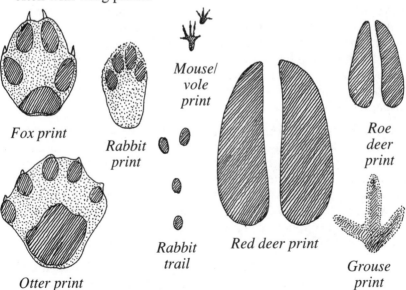

Fox print

Rabbit print

Mouse/vole print

Otter print

Rabbit trail

Red deer print

Roe deer print

Grouse print

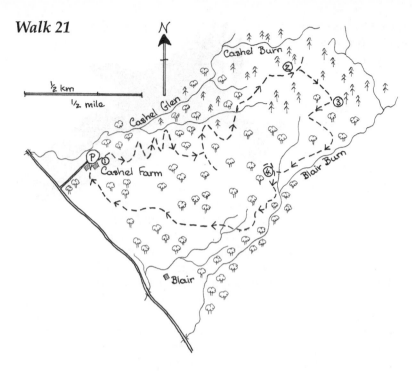

1. Leave the car park by the top right corner, following the green trail waymarkers. At a cross of tracks, go ahead. Ignore the Donald Dewar trail and carry on. Climb the pleasingly contoured way which makes three distinct zigzags as it ascends. Pause as you go to look over Loch Lomond and the hills beyond to see the mountains on Arran. Where the well marked red route leads off right, wind round left along a large curve. The way continues upwards, passing through heather.

2. As you near the moorland plateau, with hills beyond, be alert for the waymark directing you, right, off the main track, and along a delightful path over heather moorland, with little clumps of immature Scots pine thriving on hummocks on the moor. Ahead stands Conic Hill. Take the short diversion on the right for a good view over the valley below, where you can see the route taken by the red trail. From here you might spot black grouse rising up and flying over the heather.

3. Carry on along the path as it begins to bear right and descend. It comes close to the Blair Burn as it noisily races through its deep birch-lined narrow valley. On either side of the path flourish scattered rowan, juniper and birch. Go on down close beside a deer fence and then follow the path as it swings away from it. It then winds back towards the fence as it goes on descending. Finally it curves, right, away from the burn and drops down, passing, on the left, the ruins of old shielings on a flat, grassy shelf. Shielings were often found in pairs and they were used for sleeping in or for storage of milking utensils for the cattle being fattened up on the good pasture found on the flatter high land. Carry on down to join the red trail.

4. Turn left and carry on steeply down and then along the contouring path as it begins to cut right, with good views of the Loch Lomond and its several tree-clad islands. Pass through a gap in a sturdy wall and then walk beside it for a short distance. The path climbs a little before descending again. Finally the way levels out and takes you back to the parking area behind Cashel farm.

Field vole

Practicals

Type of walk: A very satisfactory route to over 1000ft/300m using a good track. The way then traverses high heather moorland from where there are excellent views. The return route takes you down across the lower slopes, with more fine views to enjoy.

Distance: 4 miles/6.5km
Time: 3 hours
Maps: OS Explorer 347, OS Landranger 56

Inchcailloch

Park in the large car park at Balmaha, grid ref 421909. To reach this take the B837 west from Drymen.

Loch Lomond's **Inchcailloch** stands just off Balmaha, one of a line of islands that lie athwart the Highland boundary fault. The name means 'island of the old woman'. Inchcailloch has been associated with religion for over 1,000 years. In the early eighth century, the Irish saint, Kentigena, daughter of the Prince of Leinster, lived and died on the island. She had once lived a secular life and had a son, but when her husband died she moved to the island and lived as a nun. In 1903 a skeleton was found, sealed under a slab of white sandstone, in front of what had been an altar. This was interpreted as the saint's grave. About the ruins of the thirteenth century church lie gravestones carved with symbols marking the crafts of the people living on the island.

Inchcailloch from Balmaha

1. Return to the road, which you cross to walk into Balmaha boatyard. Follow the metalled way round the boat sheds and boats to the ticket office. Pay your fare for the ferry before continuing to the jetty. Cross the exciting small stretch of water to land on a wooden jetty on the north-east shore of the island. Walk north (right) for a

Walk 22

Church (rems)
Balmaha
B837
Ferry (?)
Loch Lomond
Inchcailloch
The Kitchen
o Crannog
Port Bawn
Clairinch
N
½ Km
½ mile

few paces and then climb steps on the left. Continue through the glorious oak woodland, with an extensive understorey of wood rush, until you reach the next information board where you turn right and climb more steps. At the top bear right to come to the burial ground.

2. After enjoying this tranquil corner return to the entrance and walk on past the steps you climbed earlier. Go on along the pleasing grassy path and descend more steps from where you have a good view of Loch Lomond. At the Y-junction bear right to see the foundations of an old farmhouse. Then follow a narrow path down to the shore for a superb view of Conic Hill and Ben Lomond and its acolytes. Walk back up the path and at the ruins of the farmhouse, turn right to rejoin the low level path. Continue where it winds round left, remaining parallel with the shore, from where you can see more islands in the loch. Follow the path as it climbs and then after a short descent, bear right, to a derelict jetty on this south-west shore of the island.

Mallards

89

From this pleasing corner you might spot Canada geese, common gulls and goosanders.

3. Return to the main path and walk on across the camping site, passing the warden's cabin, to take a distinct track bearing left and climbing away from the little bay to a path junction at the foot of more steps on the right. Before you ascend look left to see a stone-lined kiln where grain was dried by fires. Then climb the steps and go on to pass through Scots pine, the haunt of tree creepers and where foxgloves flourish. Wander on through more scattered pines and then heather. Here there is a seat from where to enjoy the spectacular view. Look for the line of islands along the Highland Boundary Fault line. Go on up, crossing railway sleepers covered with chicken wire (to avoid slipping) to take you up on to the summit, Tom na Nigheanan.

4. You will want to pause here. Then begin your descent down more sleepers, following a path that leads to another seat, with a view over the loch to Balmaha. Follow the terraced path as it winds round the steep hillside and then go on down and down. After descending more steps, and crossing a wet area on duckboards, turn right at the next waymark, to descend to the shore and the jetty.

Treecreeper

Practicals

Type of walk: This idyllic walk should not be missed. It can be enjoyed by all the family; youngsters will like the ferry ride and the total freedom. Adults will delight in the beauty of the vegetation and the bird life. All will appreciate the peace and quiet. About the island there are many steps, well made, unobtrusive and helpful to walkers.

Distance: 1 ³/₄ miles/3km
Time: 1–2 hours
Maps: OS Explorer 347, OS Landranger 56

Conic Hill

Park in the public car park, grid ref 421909, in the village of Balmaha. To reach this take the B837, west, from Drymen.

Conic Hill is a fine grassy ridge, with several summits, the highest being 1975ft/385m. It can be seen from many places around and from its top the views are almost as dramatic as from Ben Lomond. Do not attempt this walk for a four-week period through April and May as the route from above Creityhall farm is closed because of lambing. No dogs are allowed on the hill at any time.

Conic Hill

1. Turn left out of the car park and walk the widish pavement beside the B837, which is quite quiet in winter but can be busy with visitors in the summer. The road soon leaves the houses behind and moves out into fine countryside, with woodland and then pastures on either side. The pavement, part of the West Highland Way (WHW), continues for 1 ³/₄ miles through more woodland before reaching the outskirts of Milton of Buchanan. Still on the good pavement

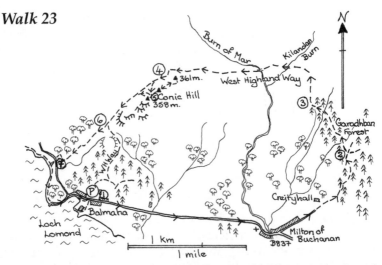

look for a fine church and then the village hall, both on the other side of the road. Beyond, look left, to see the restored waterwheel, on the side of a house, which was once a mill. Carry on to a left turn, just before a phone box and a bus shelter, to walk a short metalled way, Creityhall Road. Then the way continues as a track (WHW) leaving the houses behind and goes on to pass, on your left, the attractive farmhouse of Creityhall. Continue into a conifer plantation, which is the beginning of Garadh Ban Forest, still gently climbing, to a signposted cross of tracks and the noticeboard about lambing.

2. Turn left here and press on along the well arrowed way on a wide, sturdily reinforced track. It soon winds right and then left and enters the trees of Garadh Ban Wood. There are primroses along the banks in spring. The wide track ends at a turning place and a narrower, arrowed way carries on through the plantation. Pass through a clearing and then on along a pine-needle carpeted path to a stile out of the trees.

3. Go on along the track as it moves on through rough pasture, with a wall away to the right. Climb the next stile with Conic Hill now towering above you, to the left. Descend to cross a footbridge over a small stream, the Kilandan Burn, and go on to climb a stile. Continue along the path to begin a gentle descent into a wooded gully through which flows the birch-lined Burn of Mar. This is a very pretty corner, where you might see goldcrests slipping through

Goldcrest

the branches of trees. Cross the footbridge and then climb the slope beyond, on steps. At the top of the slope a terraced path continues. It then begins to climb steadily, with Ben Lomond coming into view. Follow the path as it starts to winds round left from where you can glimpse Loch Lomond.

4. The gradient eases and the path runs along a terrace on the north-west side of the hill, below the top. Look for the path that appears a few metres up the slope on your left and walk a few steps to join it and ascend. Soon the little path becomes a wider grassy way. Continue to the ridge and, at a meeting of paths, turn left. Climb up the first hill, and descend a little before climbing to the summit of the north easterly top of the ridge, 361m, and enjoy the superb view.

5. Return to the meeting of paths and this time go ahead up the slope to the next summit, a grassy pebbly small plateau, 358m. Then return once more to the meeting of paths, go down your ascent path for a few metres and take an easy-to-miss path dropping gently, left, which leads you easily down to the main path. Carry on left down to the Bealach Ard, where the WHW swings left.

6. Here go straight ahead along a green path that keeps to the tops of a series of gently rolling knolls, each one lower than the one before. When the ridge path seems to finish, follow a little path right to join an equally pleasing one coming in on your right and walk on. At the edge of the last hillock and, after such a glorious walk, the surface of the path changes. It drops steeply down a path of red soil, which requires care, especially if the earth is wet. It goes on down, where some careful scrambling is required. Finally the path leads into pleasing deciduous woodland. As it nears the valley the way becomes awkward, this time very wet for a short distance. Once you have crossed a stream it continues as a dry path to a gate to the minor road, west of Balmaha.

7. Cross and go through a gate on the right of two, or climb the gate on the left. Walk across the pasture to join the WHW and turn left to walk into woodland and then continue along the shoreline path constructed to celebrate the Millennium. Stroll on the lovely way below towering cliffs. Cross the fine Millennium bridge and go on to walk the metalled way to come to the foot of the Pass of Balmaha. Stroll on the paved way, with a wall to the left and the lake beyond. Walk through the village of Balmaha to the car park on the left.

Cloudberry

Practicals

Type of walk: Enjoyably challenging, over a fine hill, with a pleasing shoreline return. Some unavoidable road walking. The final descent requires care on the slope and through the stretch of wet woodland. Well motivated youngsters will like this walk.

Distance: 7 ½ miles/12km
Time: 4–5 hours
Maps: OS Explorer 347, OS Landranger 56 and 57

24

Killearn and Endrick Water

Park in the car park in the village of Killearn, grid ref 523862. This lies on the west side of the A875, where it is joined by B834, and where there are toilets.

The oldest references to **Killearn** are in thirteenth century documents relating to the Earls of Lennox, though the lands around were later associated with the Grahams who held them until the mid-eighteenth century. After 1760, Sir James Montgomery built a planned village here, using the existing cottages around the church as its nucleus. Killearn was an important staging post for Highland black cattle on their way to the tryst at Falkirk. The village also had a thriving weaving industry, with flax grown locally. The growth of power-loom weaving, in factories, led to a decline in home weaving.

Endrick Bridge

George Buchanan, 1506–82, was born at the Moss, Killearn, and became one of the leading humanist thinkers and reformer of the age. He was also a linguist and scholarly writer, as well as tutor to King James VI. The Buchanan monument stands 31m high and was erected in 1788. It towers high, just south of the parish church.

Walk 24

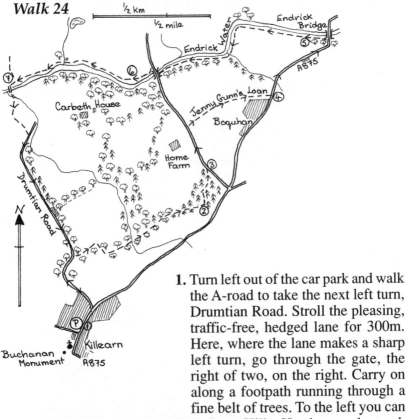

1. Turn left out of the car park and walk the A-road to take the next left turn, Drumtian Road. Stroll the pleasing, traffic-free, hedged lane for 300m. Here, where the lane makes a sharp left turn, go through the gate, the right of two, on the right. Carry on along a footpath running through a fine belt of trees. To the left you can see Conic Hill and, beyond, the Luss Hills. Head on as the track winds right and then left. The way then runs along the edge of Glen Wood, with a fenced pasture to your right. Follow the path as it weaves on through the trees, ignoring gates and stiles out of this shelter belt between two pastures and go on into woodland.

2. At a wide grassy ride, turn left, along it. Then, well before a fenced pasture and by a post, take, on your right, an occasionally indistinct path, leading into conifers. Follow it as it goes over a tiny bank, on

the left, and go on winding left to continue through the plantation to its end where you join the road to Balfron Station.

3. Turn left and stroll on to just beyond Home farm. Here take a track on the right, known as Jenny Gunn's Loan. Carry on the pleasing way, lined with oak and young beech and fenced on either side as it passes through pastures. Eventually it becomes gravelled as it continues in front of several houses, on the edge of Boquhan, and comes to the side of the A875 once more.

4. Turn left and walk the pavement and when this runs out, cross with care, to walk the pavement on the opposite side. Go on until you reach the start of Endrick Bridge. Cross the A-road to take a track that carries on beneath an avenue of beech, beside the fine Endrick Water, on your right. Pause here to look back at the superb sandstone bridge and also be alert for a flash of petrol blue as this is the haunt of a kingfisher. Stroll on along the avenue until you descend, a little right, to the side of the river, to avoid trampling the farmer's field of silage grass.

5. Walk on the glorious path beside the hurrying river. In high summer this becomes a floral highway. Go on as the river curves gently left, watching out for herons, dippers, grey wagtails and possibly another kingfisher. Walk on along the river bank before moving into woodland, with a few trees between you and the water. Pass under an aqueduct and a road bridge and go through a stone arch to pass under the old road bridge. Then wind, left, up steps to join the side of the road to Balfron Station once more. Turn left and walk the old road over the bridge to take a farm gate on the left. Wind left to return to the side of the river now on your left, with pastures to your right.

Greater bellflower

97

6. As you stroll on you might see oyster catchers and redshank near a pool in the middle of the pasture. And then the path comes to the side of a small burn emptying its water into the river. Here, step over the wire on your right and drop down (or slide down on your seat) to cross the stream on a large stepping stone and then climb up the other side. If the burn is in spate, move right, upstream, to find an easier crossing place. Continue on by the river along a more overgrown section of the path where very soon you need to keep above the alders lining the Endrick Water. Take care where the electrified fence comes right up to the side of the path. If you find this rather daunting, or the river is high, go back to take a stile, over the fence, just before the electrification starts, and walk in the pasture, remaining parallel with the river to go through a gate onto a track. Turn left to join the riverside path, where there are seats.

7. Walk on to cross the elegant footbridge and go up the hedged lane to a T-junction. Turn right on to the metalled lane and walk for nearly a kilometre, to reach the A-road at Killearn. Turn right to return to the car park.

Kingfisher

Practicals

Type of walk: A superb riverside walk, reached by pleasing hedged footpaths and quiet lanes, with a little walking along the A875.

Distance: 5 miles/8km
Time: 2–3 hours
Maps: OS Explorer 348, OS Landranger 57

25

Dunmore from Fintry

Park in front of the village hall at Fintry, grid ref 616867. This lies on the north side of the road, just before a junction of roads in the centre of the village. To reach Fintry, leave the A875, south of Balfron, and take the B818, east.

Newtown of Fintry was set up on the site of the present day Fintry, in 1794, by Peter Speirs of Culcreuch Castle, as a model village for workers in his cotton mill. The houses on the south side of the main road were the original mill workers' dwellings. Alas the mill failed in 1844.

In 1679 the local covenanters held a conventicle or open air religious meeting on Dunmore Hill, overlooking the village. There they were attacked and dispersed by soldiers from the Stirling garrison. This spot is known as the **covenanters' hole**.

Village hall, Fintry

1. Cross the road from the parking area and walk left (east) towards the fine drinking fountain in the middle of the road junction. Carry on to turn right into Quarry Road. Climb gently uphill and at the start of Dunmore Gardens, turn right,

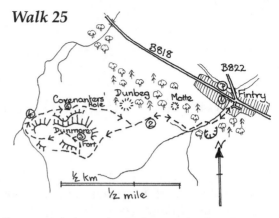

Walk 25

as directed by a small arrowed sign, along the continuing Quarry Road. Walk on to bear right in front of a house, and then left, to go on along a rising hedged track, passing the disused quarry. Ford the burn and walk up beside it to a tied gate. Climb round the left side of the gate and move out into a pasture. Wind right along a wide, raised, grassy track in the direction of Dunmore Hill.

2. Head on along the track as it curves left and climbs steeply. Ignore narrow paths going off left and right, the latter your return route. Carry on up the very steep path to pass a great tumble of boulders below crags. Among these ferns and scattered trees thrive. When you reach the brow you can spot two rocky tops ahead. Toil on up beside a derelict wall on your right. Then at the corner of two ancient walls, pass through on to grassy slopes. Follow the path as it winds round right and then, almost immediately, when the slopes of the hill to your right become gentler, leave the path and climb up right. Pass through boulders and then bear slightly left, up to a huge pile of stones, the site of an ancient iron-age fort.

3. From here wind left along the elongated summit of the plateau, which is grassy with outcropping rocks. Enjoy the fine view ahead as you go. At the edge of the plateau, look for a grassy slope down which to begin your descent. Very soon, wind left below crags and then bear right, to continue along a groove or sunken way (possibly an ancient track), keeping to the right of a lower hill. Follow the groove downhill with Ben Lomond slightly to the left. The groove leads you to the edge of a steep-sided ravine. Here a fence starts and stretches across the slopes, with a little path running just above it, along which you continue.

100

4. Go through a gap in a derelict wall and then move away from the fence to pass under the awesome, sheer, craggy, basalt face of Dunmore. Keep roughly on the same contour as you climb a little hillock and carry on the now clearer path, which traverses the hillside. It then leads into a large oval-shaped hollow, with a tiny hillock in its middle. This is the convenanters' hole. It looks so easy to hide in and it cannot be seen from below.

5. Follow the path as it leads left over the lip of the hollow and continue on, keeping parallel with woodland just below. Look through the trees to see Dunbeg, another fort. Carry on the now good path to reach the wider path, taken on your climb up Dunmore. Here you might spot the pointed ears of a hare as it crouches in the grass. Turn left and descend by your outward route to return to the village.

Brown hare

Practicals

Type of walk: Short and quite delightful but the ascent, on a good path, is very steep as it climbs to the first brow.

Distance: 2 ½ miles/4 km
Time: 1 ½ hours
Maps: OS Explorer 348, OS Landranger 57

26

Gargunnock

Park in the main street of the village of Gargunnock, opposite the village inn, grid ref 70593945. This lies on the south side of the A811, Stirling to Dumbarton road, 4 miles west of Stirling.

Lady Younger of the Younger family of brewing fame was out walking her dogs by the Leckie burn when one became entangled in a thicket of rhododendrons. She went to rescue it and noticed a strangely carved rock in the bushes. She passed the information to archaeologists in Glasgow and the resulting excavation uncovered the remains of a substantial **broch**, of a type similar to those found

Waterfall below Downie's Loup

in the Northern Isles. It appeared to have been destroyed very suddenly and material in use at the time was abandoned on the latest floor and buried. As a result Leckie has yielded a large proportion of equipment of a well off, broch-owning family in the second century AD.

Downie's Loup is a fine waterfall, one of many cascading from the basalt plateau of the Campsie Fells, here called the Gargunnock Hills. Downie was a horseman who tried to leap the fall on his horse. Rumour has it that he was killed at the 3rd attempt.

Walk 26

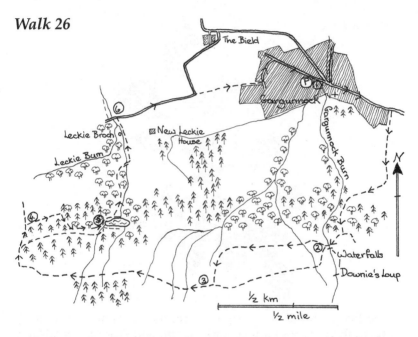

1. Walk east down the main street, cross a footbridge beside the narrow road bridge over the Gargunnock Burn and turn right to climb the road, going uphill, past the church. Just before the de-restriction sign, take a track, on the right, signed 'To the Hill'. Once past a few cottages there is a padlocked gate, with a stile beside it, which you take. Continue up the track to climb the next stile, beside an unlocked gate, and continue along the side of a small burn, its banks covered with foxgloves in high summer. Soon wind right on the track to cross a pasture to a gate and then walk on into a wood. Wind left and begin to climb again under splendid old beech trees

to reach a gate and a stile at the top of the wood. Beyond, turn right at the T-junction and carry on through scattered shrubs, especially wild rose, gorse and hawthorn. Pause here and look high on the hill, ahead and slightly left, to see the waterfall, Downie's Loup.

2. There is another fine fall just above the ford where the track crosses the burn. Go up the far bank and continue straight ahead, following a tractor track across a field to a gate and on across the next field. The views to the right are splendid. Cross the next burn on an earth bank over a culvert. Here, where the tractor track ends, walk

Wild roses

up the hill with the wall to your right and the burn, in its deep gully, to the left. Join a waymarked path and cross the wall by a sturdy ladderstile. Once across there are no more waymarks.

3. Walk straight ahead, easily negotiating more small gullies, across a pleasant flowery grassland with occasional rushy patches. When you can see a plantation of young trees ahead, turn downhill and head for its lower corner, to pick up a clear sheep trod. Go through a gap in a derelict wall and continue on the trod below the plantation until it becomes a good reinforced track. Pass through a gate. Walk on until the track turns downhill and goes through a gate into woodland, the way fenced on either side.

4. Carry on down the track and into the field below the wood. Turn right to walk along the top of the field. At the far end there is a very difficult stile over the fence on the right; it has a very high step and wire complete with unprotected barbs. Cross the small open space beyond, with a fine wall on your left. When you reach the trees go round the end of the wall, watching out for bits of old fence. Then walk below a row of superb beech trees standing proud on top of a ha-ha (a raised bank). Cross a small burn and 50m farther on leave the ha-ha and join a forest track on the left.

5. Go left along the track and in a short distance look through the trees, on your right, to see a pleasing tranquil pool. Then take, on the left, a waymarked permitted path, which at first descends quite steeply. It passes through open birch woodland and then beech, finally passing through a rhododendron 'tunnel'. Cross a burn on an old stone bridge and at the edge of the wood turn left to descend inside the wall, with the burn to your left. The large house across the fields is New Leckie House, home of the Younger family. Look among the dense vegetation on the left of the path, beyond the burn, to see if you can spot the stones of the Leckie Broch. Continue down the path to go through two kissing gates to join a minor road.

6. Turn right and walk in the direction of Gargunnock. Where the road turns acute left go ahead on a footpath on top of a bank, lined by large trees. Enjoy a pause on a bench from where you can admire the view back to the escarpment. Then continue on behind garden fences, and on to a road among new houses. Turn left and, at the next junction, turn right to walk downhill to your car.

Practicals

Type of walk: A pleasant walk with superb views below the escarpment of the Gargunnock Hills. There is one difficult stile. Watch out for notices about pheasant shooting, October to February.

Distance:	5 miles/8km
Time:	2 ½–3 hours
Maps:	OS Explorer 348, OS Landranger 57

27

Campsie Glen and Cort-ma Law

Park in the village of Clachan of Campsie, grid ref 611796. This is reached by a turn, north, off the A891 at Haughhead, 2 miles west of Lennoxtown.

A few steps north of the parking area lies the graveyard of old **St Machan's church**. It took its name from St Machan, who brought Christianity to Campsie during the Dark Ages. After travels in Ireland and Italy, he erected a small chapel at the foot of the Glen and used an adjacent well for baptisms. On his death, he was buried at the site and the first parish church was erected over his grave around 1175.

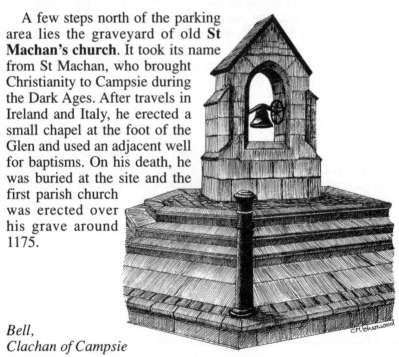

Bell,
Clachan of Campsie

1. From the parking area follow the signpost for 'Campsie Glen and waterfalls'. Turn left round the last building and walk on along a pleasing track, where you might spot several carved faces on the

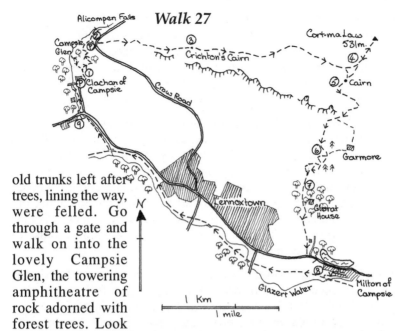

Walk 27

old trunks left after trees, lining the way, were felled. Go through a gate and walk on into the lovely Campsie Glen, the towering amphitheatre of rock adorned with forest trees. Look for several pretty waterfalls, then return along the path and take, on your left, another path that zigzags up the fell to ease the gradient. To your left lies the glen and as you climb you have ever improving views over Strathblane. Pause on the seat at the viewpoint and then go on up to pass through a kissing gate.

2. Beyond, bear left to descend steps into a deep ravine to see the spectacular falls of Alicompen. In spate they are magnificent. Then climb the steps to regain the track and turn left, soon to pass through another kissing gate. Follow the track to the upper car park, which is reached by Crow Road from Lennoxtown. (For this ramble it is better to use the lower car park to avoid the climb through the glen at the end of a long walk.) Go through the car park and cross Crow Road, with care, and press on up a wide grassy trod. There are several paths to choose from but make sure you take one that continues uphill. Climb steadily the delightful green sward to come to Crichton's Cairn where you will want to pause to enjoy the views.

3. From the cairn look ahead to see the next one and then stroll the continuing path, which gently rises and descends as it crosses the high plateau, with Strathblane and the Clyde Valley to your right. Carry on along the erosion-free way over the extensive moorland,

107

eventually to descend a little to a stile over the boundary fence. Then climb again through the mat and deer grass. Go on past a small cairn enjoying, in summer, the carolling of skylarks and meadow pipits. Soon you descend to a hollow to step across a small stream and then ascend again. Ignore the next two right turns off the main path—but note the second one which is walked later.

4. Follow the main path as it swings left and climbs steadily. Cross a footbridge of sleepers, then step across the next stream and ascend easily to the trig point on Cort-ma- Law (531m). Enjoy the grand view north of Lecket Hill and more of the rolling Campsie Fells. Then return from the summit to cross the stream and the sleeper footbridge. Ignore your outward path and go on ahead along the narrower path noted earlier. This leads to a cairn seen ahead close to the edge of the escarpment, where you will want to pause to look down on the fine valley below.

5. Then take the path, south-west, descending gently over the edge of the escarpment and on down to a gate. Beyond, follow a narrow path swinging left. It levels for a distance and then descends to a cross of tracks. Go over the cross and on down a rather rough way (there is an easier path on the right banking of the track) and follow it as it winds right. Go on down to come to a gully, on the right, softened by ferns, ash and ivy and where you might spot a stoat. Descend the track for a few more steps as it swings left and then leave it, right, to go through a gate into a pasture. Drop straight down to go through the next gate and on to pass through a third gate.

6. Walk the continuing track that winds left to join a track from Garmore farm, along which you turn right. Where this reinforced track swings right, on a zigzag, head down the green sward to cut off a large bend to arrive at a lower corner on the track. Cross the track and drop down another grassy way and continue alongside a wood on your left. Then bear right on a track, avoid a wet patch and head on along a fenced way beside a delightful pond. Stride on to rejoin the reinforced track once more and turn left.

7. Walk to the right of a crenellated house and on through a glorious bluebell wood. Emerge from the trees and carry on between pastures to arrive at the A891. Turn left and stroll the pavement for a quarter of a mile into Milton of Campsie. When you can spot a right turn, Valleyfield, cross the A-road, with care, and walk down this side

turn. Turn right, immediately at the T-junction, and then take a footpath from the turning space at the road end descending left, through a pasture to the side of the Glazert Water. Follow the path right. Climb steps up onto the trackbed of a dismantled railway and turn right.

8. Remain on this pleasant hedged level track as it passes through pastures and then continues south of Lennoxtown. Go on over footbridges and crossing roads that bisect it for nearly two and a half miles until you reach a signpost directing you, right, along a good track to Clachan of Campsie. The pleasing path continues beside a pretty burn, the way lined with bushes, and forest trees.

9. At the end of the track, turn right along a short path to join the A-road at Haughhead. Cross, with care, and go through the splendid gates of Schoenstatt Shrine. This is a retreat and conference centre run by the Schoenstatt Sisters of Mary and is a place of pilgrimage for thousands of people each year. Just beyond the gates turn right to follow the signposted 'Woodland walk'. Cross a footbridge and go on along the charming path, through lovely woodland to cross a second footbridge. A short distance beyond, turn right to walk to another set of fine gates onto a lane. Turn right and then left to return to the car park.

Stoat in ermine

Practicals

Type of walk: A good walk of contrasts with a lush glen, a dramatic waterfall, high moorland, fine deciduous woodland and a level disused railway track.

Distance:	8 ½ miles/13.8km
Time:	4–5 hours
Maps:	OS Explorer 348, OS Landranger 64

28

Loch Ardinning

Park on the east side of the A81 about 2km south of Strathblane, in a large lay-by edged with sandstone blocks, grid ref 563777. This is reached by the A81 from Glasgow to Aberfoyle.

Loch Ardinning is a natural loch formed in a shallow basin, with sandstone and conglomerate to the north-east and basalt outcrops to the south-west. It has a substantial area of open water where ducks may be seen at most times of the year but especially in winter, and a good vegetation succession with sedge fen, reedbed and willow carr. A small dam was built across the outflow in 1796 to raise the water level in order to supply power to the mills in Strathblane. Because the loch is about 400ft/120m above sea level it freezes regularly in winter and so was a popular curling loch. The remains of the building where curling stones were stored can be seen on the walk. The loch and surrounding wood and moorland now belong to the Scottish Wildlife Trust who manage it with the aim of maintaining and increasing the diversity of habitats for the benefit of the wildlife.

Loch Ardinning

1. Take the raised path from the back of the lay-by, which runs parallel with the main road through willow carr. At the reserve entrance turn right, away from the road, crossing a small dam. Look for bullrushes and, in summer, the delicate

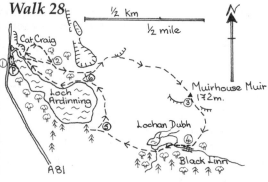

lilac spires of water plantain in the pools to your right. You might see reed buntings and, with luck, a heron standing patiently at the edge of the reeds. Go past the interpretative board and on along the nature trail, a good level path, recently surfaced and which is suitable for wheelchair use. Carry on past a small quarry on your left and then, beyond a rather fine small crag take the left branch at a Y-junction. Walkers can climb a steep unsurfaced path which comes to the top of the crag; wheelchair users and those feeling idle can continue up the surfaced path and turn left at the top of the bank to come back to the top of the crag, where the two paths rejoin. This is Cat Craig. Press on round the main path enjoying the fine view of the Campsie Fells with Dumgoyne prominent on the end.

2. At the next junction turn left. There is a large disused quarry on the left. Loch Ardinning is below to the right, in a shallow depression surrounded by open birch and pine woods. At a kissing gate the wheelchair path turns right, but this walk continues through the gate. Turn left beyond it and walk uphill beside the wall until it turns away to the left. Continue towards a solitary oak tree, where there is a conveniently placed seat facing the view. The path follows the ridge above Strathblane, looking over to the escarpment of the Campsies. The little hill below is Dunglass, a volcanic plug. Follow the path past another small quarry to a bench, and turn right with the main path towards a cairn on the highest point of Muirhouse Muir, from where there is a splendid view.

3. Beyond the cairn the obvious path goes on downhill and continues as a grassy trod through bracken. It is now marked with tall red-topped poles, waymarkers that take you all the way back to the nature trail. Cross the hillside to enter birch woodland, where a burn flows through a narrow ravine in a series of pretty waterfalls, the Black Linn.

4. Turn right and follow the bank downstream. Cross a wooden footbridge. The reedy lochan on the right, seen through the birch trees, is Lochan Dubh, but the path keeps away from it and follows the edge of a gully down towards a wall. Cross another footbridge over the outflow from the lochan, where it goes through the wall, and carry on with the wall to your left. The path can be very marshy after rain. Cross an indistinct track and then wet moor, where purple moor grass grows.

5. Before the path crosses a stile into pine trees, turn right downhill on another clear path towards the head of Loch Ardinning, still following the waymarkers. Go round the head of the loch, where again the path can be wet, and then through new tree plantings above the shore to come to a kissing gate into woodland.

6. Beyond turn left to rejoin the nature trail wheelchair path, which continues just above the loch shore. Here at the right time of year you might see goldeneye, tufted duck, mallard and goosander. Look for the concrete slab on the right, which is all that remains of the brick building where curling stones used to be stored. Rejoin your approach path below Cat Craig and walk to the entrance and then to the parking area.

Goosanders

Practicals

Type of walk: Clear paths all the way. The nature trail by Loch Ardinning is suitable for wheelchairs but the moorland paths are rough and in some places very wet.

Distance: 2 ½ miles/4km
Time: 1–2 hours.
Maps: OS Explorer 348, OS Landranger 64

29

Mugdock Castle and Craigallian Loch

Park at the Mugdock Country Park Visitor Centre, grid ref 547781, where there are toilets and a good cafe. Remember to note the time the car park is locked at the end of the day. To reach the Park, leave Glasgow by the A81, north, and, beyond Milngavie, take the second left following the signs for the Country Park.

Craigend Castle was built in 1816 as a mansion rather than a castle. It was turretted and decorated in 'Scots Baronial' style and belonged, in turn, to various wealthy businessmen. The last owner had a zoo in the grounds, which failed in 1956, and after that the building fell into ruin.

The fourteenth century **Mugdock Castle**, in contrast to Craigend Castle, was built as a stronghold, situated on a rocky hill and almost surrounded by loch and marsh. It

Mugdock Castle

belonged to the Grahams, who later acquired the lands of the Earldom of Lennox, making the Duke of Montrose the biggest landowner in the area until after the 1914–1918 war. Today only two of the four towers of the castle remain, but one has been restored so that visitors can see what it was like inside.

The **Carbeth Huts** were built from the time of the depression in the 1930s until after the 1939–45 war, on rented land. They were considered as an affordable way for people to get out of Glasgow at weekends. Some of these huts can be seen scattered among the trees around Carbeth Loch.

Walk 29

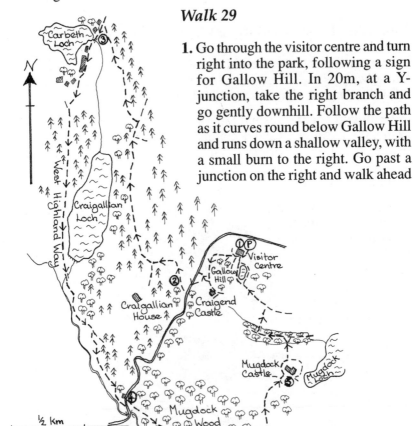

1. Go through the visitor centre and turn right into the park, following a sign for Gallow Hill. In 20m, at a Y-junction, take the right branch and go gently downhill. Follow the path as it curves round below Gallow Hill and runs down a shallow valley, with a small burn to the right. Go past a junction on the right and walk ahead to look at the ruins of Craigend Castle, which appear through the trees. The ruins are dangerous and should not be entered. Retrace your steps to the junction, now on the left. Go over a bridge and across the field ahead to a gap in the wall, which borders the road. Turn left and walk for 140m to take a path on the right with a Scottish Rights of Way Society sign to Cuilt Braes.

2. Follow the path downhill and turn left at the bottom. Go with it as it continues over level ground to a T-junction. Bear right and walk on through tall conifers. Soon the ground on the right becomes open but it will not remain so for long as it has been replanted and surrounded with a deer fence. Ahead you can see the escarpment of the Campsies, with Dumgoyne on the left, through huge ancient beeches growing among spruce. At the end of the deer fence ignore the track which branches right and go on for 100m to take the left fork. This leads slightly uphill, still with a line of beech beside you. The track soon begins to descend, slanting down the hillside into a lower valley. Behind to your left, is Craigallian Loch, and ahead is the smaller Carbeth Loch, with its scattering of wooden huts and chalets. Beyond the fields and woods Ben Lomond, and its associated jumble of mountains, rise dramatically.

3. At the bottom of the track, cross a stile and turn left onto the West Highland Way (WHW). Carry on down past the chalets to cross the burn flowing out of Carbeth Loch, where you might spot tufted duck and goldeneye. Then climb steadily, ignoring tracks going right to service the huts. Continue on the WHW as it runs along the hillside above reed-fringed Craigallian Loch, which is set in a wooded basin, with the large Craigallian House on the far hillside. Goosanders and mute swans idle on the waters of the loch. Cross the outflow burn and then continue parallel with it, with wooded

Tufted ducks

rocky outcrops to your left and a wet valley to your right. The burn joins another and becomes the Allander Water, fast-flowing and alder-lined. In spring and summer the valley bottom is colourful with irises and meadowsweet. The track goes up through trees towards Craigallian House; at this point take a footpath to the right, with a WHW waymark, which carries on round the edge of the fen. Finally it goes uphill through more trees to emerge on to a minor road near a cottage.

4. Walk left and after 30m take a path on the right, which passes between impressive gateposts into Mugdock Wood. The trees are old oak and birch, with lots of honeysuckle. Here you might see long-tailed tits, treecreepers and goldcrests foraging among the branches. At the next Y-junction leave the WHW and take the left branch, signed 'visitor centre'. Carry on uphill along a wooded shelf, with low cliffs to your left and, in winter, a distant glimpse of Glasgow. Join a path coming in from the right and notice, on your left, the remains of a woodman's cottage. The path climbs gently across an open area of scattered deciduous trees, then crosses a wet hollow on duckboards. Climb the stepped way at the far side to an intricate stone stile and then cross the open ground beyond. The ruins of Mugdock castle rise through the trees ahead.

5. Explore the castle and then go down either side of it to take a boardwalk across a bog. Turn left and left again, immediately, onto a reinforced track, signed to the 'visitor centre'. Take the next turn on the right to cross a burn followed by open grassland, and turn left on the path before low cliffs at the far side. This brings you to a small pond in front of the visitor centre.

Practicals

Type of walk: A very satisfactory walk. Good paths and tracks all the way, most of them surfaced.

Distance: 5 miles/8km
Time: 2–3 hours
Maps: OS Explorer 348, OS Landranger 64

Blanefield

From Monday to Saturday you can park behind St Kessog's Roman Catholic Church, grid ref 556797, Blanefield, where a contribution to the upkeep of the garden would be much appreciated. On Sundays you will have to make use of the town's very limited roadside parking. To reach Blanefield, leave Glasgow by the A81. Just past the town's Spar shop, on the left of the A-road, turn right in front of the very obvious war memorial. Beyond the memorial is the drive leading up to the parking area.

In 1867 the **Blane valley railway** was opened for passengers. It was hoped that this would entice Glasgow's wealthy businessmen to build their houses in Strathblane and use the line to commute. But this did not happen. The line took a circuitous route to Glasgow and traffic was always light. In 1951, passenger services were withdrawn and, in 1959, the line was closed. The **West Highland Way**, traversed on this walk, now takes you along a section of the disused railway track. Beside the track runs the pipeline, under a grassy bank, that carries water from Loch Lomond to Central Scotland.

Glengoyne distillery

117

1. From the parking area return to the road and turn right to begin a gentle climb along a 'no through road' which, beyond a gate, continues as a track. As you stroll look for small sturdy buildings which service the water pipeline from Loch Katrine to Glasgow. This was installed after a serious outbreak of cholera in the city and was opened by Queen Victoria in 1859. Continue on along the easy-to-walk track, which passes below the towering, tiered, dramatic ridge of Black Craig. Ahead, and on the right, are the volcanic plugs of Dumfoyn and then Dumgoyne. Go on to pass through scattered birch and alder woodland, where in early spring the trees are laden with catkins. After 1½km from the start go through a kissing gate and pass a single storey white dwelling, (Cantywheery). Cross an iron bridge, patterned with a border of roses, and climb a little before winding left and then curving right as it descends. The way is glorious with Dumgoyne at your back and a deep ravine to your left, with a tall ventilation chamber for the aqueduct among the trees.

2. Continue on the winding track which begins to descend and passes a cottage on the right. Ignore a wide track going off left and walk ahead through conifer woodland. Follow the lovely path as it carries on under the deciduous trees of Parkhill Woods to pass, on the left, another smaller spectacular tree-clad volcanic plug. Once out of the trees press on along the pleasing track, with Dumgoyne towering up to your right. Watch out for where the way divides. Here, take the left branch and cut across the corner of parkland to go through a gate into Scots pine.

118

3. Go on down and through more trees to peer, right, over the parapet of a small bridge to see the deep drop below, where its rocky sides have been smoothed by the burn when in spate. As you leave the trees you have a wonderful view of Ben Lomond. Continue on down to join the A81, which you should cross with care. Turn left and walk along the verge for a few steps then pause in front of fine, white Glen Goyne Distillery, which you might wish to visit and take a tasting! Opposite the distillery are rows of bonded warehouses, the whisky piped to them under the road.

4. Turn right, off the A-road, to walk between the storage buildings and continue through a gate onto a track. This bears slightly right across a pasture to join the West Highland Way (WHW), which you can access by two gates or a stile. Turn left and begin your stroll on the pleasing trackway of the old Blane Valley railway. To your right is the raised bank below which flows the water pipeline. Cross a lane by using two interesting stiles and, at the next lane, follow the WHW as it continues to the right along it. Soon the WHW moves over to the side of the fence, on the right, and then carries on past a house to a stile.

5. Beyond, descend a slope and follow the path as it winds left, and climbs steadily, passing below another volcanic plug, splendid Dumgoyach. Once beyond the hill, look across (but don't visit) to see several Neolithic standing stones on the brow of a sloping pasture. Shortly the WHW turns right and climbs a slope. Here this walk goes ahead for a few steps to a T-junction, where you turn left. Carry on to the next gated T-junction. Beyond the gate, bear right and begin to ascend the slope before descending through woodland to the B821, the road to Blanefield.

Buzzard

119

6. Descend left to pass a farm on the left and then the old station building (now a private house) on the right. Just beyond the latter take the gate on the right to continue on the old railway track once more. Eventually you need to climb a stepped way up onto the railway embankment from where there is a pleasing view of another volcanic plug, Dunglass. At a cross of tracks, turn left. Just before you reach the side of the Blane Water, bear left, cross the bridge and ascend a railed, reinforced track up to the A81, arriving opposite the war memorial. Cross and return to the parking area behind the church.

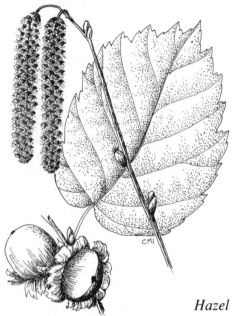

Hazel

Practicals

Type of walk: This is a glorious walk along quiet tracks, with dramatic scenery all around. Easy walking underfoot and some easy slopes to ascend.

Distance: 7 ½ miles/12km
Time: 4–5 hours
Maps: OS Explorer 348, OS Landranger 64

***NB** The pheasant shooting season is from October to February. Notices are generally in place at the start of the walk.*

Dumgoyne

Park in a large layby, on the A81, opposite Glengoyne Malt Distillery, grid ref 528827. This lies just over 3 ½ miles north-west of Strathblane.

Dumgoyne, 427m, the volcanic plug and shapely hill, seen so often during walks in this book, is the most prominent of the volcanic hills of the Strathblane Fells. Its sturdy shape entices you to climb it. It is one of the remnant volcanoes from which emerged the lavas of the Clyde plateau. The lava which solidified in the vent of the volcano became harder than the lava which flowed out, and therefore more resistant to erosion. The basalt lava flows give the Campsies their layered cliff and plateau structure. Dumgoyne and Dumfoyn, its neighbour, both contain basalt agglomerates.

Dumgoyne

1. Cross the road from the parking area and walk up the track that leads off the A-road and runs to the left of all the buildings associated with the distillery. This is a private road, with no access for vehicles or for dogs. Walk on up, with pasture to your left and mixed conifers to your right. Curve round right to pass a cottage,

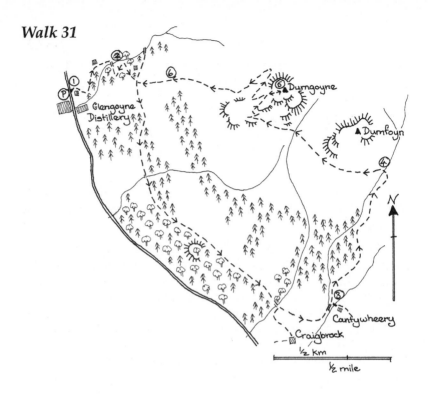

on the left, and continue with a glimpse of Dumgoyne peeping over the top of the forest trees, on the right.

2. Cross a bridge and zigzag up through the wood. Go through a gate into an open pasture, pass another cottage, on the left, and walk on beside a tall stand of Scots pine. Join a reinforced track, coming in on your left, along which you continue, right. Stroll the pleasant way through alternating open pasture and mixed woodland. As you near a gate out of the woodland, look left to see an aqueduct, another part of the architecturally pleasing network of syphon wells and inspection chambers, seen on this walk, and which carry water from Loch Katrine to thirsty Glasgow. Eventually the track winds left and here look, right, to see a fine inspection chamber for the aqueduct set in a leafy hollow. Follow the track across a metal bridge, with roses on its upright struts. Immediately beyond, take a kissing gate on the left.

3. Stride on along an easy grassy trod soon to curve right on a rising

way, with bracken on both sides and beyond, on the left, a dark plantation. At a faint Y-junction, take the left branch, a much more well-used path. Go past the corner of the plantation and then ahead as the distinct path drifts away from the trees and then continues parallel with them. In July look for ragged robin, spotted orchids and lousewort. Keep on the path as it passes through dense bracken and then winds right beside a fine tree-lined ravine through which tumbles the Craigbrock Burn. To the left you can see the Luss Hills and a tiny corner of Loch Lomond.

4. Cross the burn on convenient stones and climb to take a stile over a wall. Carry on along the grassy trod through shorter bracken, and then on a delightful terrace-like path below Dumfoyn, to your right. Here in high summer, you might see whinchats, pale-breasted and 'chat, chatting' on the top of a frond of bracken. Where the bracken ceases the grassy path goes on under Dumgoyne and then winds round right and comes to a large boulder in the centre of the now wider way. Just after the boulder, turn left and climb the slanting path to the ridge. At a contouring path, turn right. A few steps along this path, wind up left on an indistinct path to the top of the ridge to join a wide track that leads on

Ragged robin

123

to the summit of the fine hill. Pause here by the cairn and enjoy the superb panoramic view.

5. To continue, leave the top by the wide track by which you attained the summit. Go down a rocky patch and then carry on the main path that continues along the grassy ridge. Ignore the path to the right, which is steeper and more difficult to descend. At the end of the ridge turn sharply right, with the path. Descend a little, before going on along a descending traverse across the hillside. This is a pleasing path with just a few awkward steps. Then the path does a hairpin bend, left, and reaches a gentler slope. Cross the top of scree and follow the path as it makes a wide curve to come back to the bottom of the scree. Go on down to climb two stiles, with a little burn between.

6. Beyond, go slightly right across the pasture to pick up your outward route by crossing the main track steps. Bear right to walk below the Scots pines and stroll on to take the gate into the wood. Descend the track to the side of the A81 and cross to the parking layby.

Whinchat

Practicals

Type of walk: A delightful circular walk. The ascent, though always up, is gradual. The descent, much steeper, requires care. The views are excellent. Watch out for notices about pheasant shooting, October to February

Distance: 4 ½ miles/7.4km
Time: 2–3 hours
Maps: OS Explorer 348, OS Landranger 57 or 64

The Whangie

Park in the large Queen's View car park, grid ref 512808, on the left side of the road, going north. To reach this use the A809 from Glasgow to Drymen, north of Bearsden.

The Whangie is a geological phenomenon probably caused in one of two ways. It may have been formed by faulting so that part of the rock was pulled away from the rest by the movement of the earth, or by glacial plucking where the outer rocks were so firmly frozen into the glacier that when it moved they split away from the parent rock along lines of weakness and were pulled out to their present position. Legend however has it that it was formed by the devil flicking his tail as he flew over the nearby Stockie Muir on his way to host a witches' meeting.

The Whangie

Walk 32

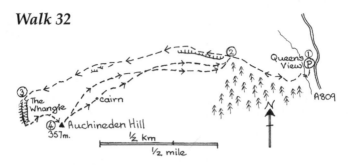

1. Leave the car park by the obvious path which curves back towards a forestry plantation. Cross a wall by a stone step stile and then follow the sleeper-reinforced path up the hillside beside the trees. The sleepers are very slippery when wet or frosted so take care. Because this walk is very popular the path beyond the sleepers is quite eroded in places; try to avoid spreading it further.

2. At the upper edge of the forest climb a ladder stile over a fence and contour round the hillside above the fence. Go on along the path, climbing gently with basalt cliffs or steep grassy slopes to your left, for nearly a mile. The view to the north is stupendous. Much of the whole area of this book is laid out there. At a Y-junction where there are interesting rocky outcrops, the Wee Whangie, it is best to take the right, lower path. Eventually the path turns a corner to the south and suddenly there are the cliffs of the Whangie ahead, guarded by a tall flake called the Gendarme.

3. There are several paths that can be followed here and it is best to allow plenty of time to explore because it is an amazing place. The best way is to take a small path up to the left which climbs into the gap between the cliff and the outer rock ridge, although if you miss this it is easy to get in a little further along. This is the most spectacular part of this walk. Through gaps in the outer wall there are views of Loch Lomond and its surrounding mountains. As you go through the gap it becomes narrower until it looks as if progress is barred; but a twist in the path brings you through a last gap and then down a rocky staircase to rejoin the lower path which went all the way round the outside. After exploring continue south along the outer path, which takes you round the corner and then up into a little valley. At the back take a steep path on the right which climbs the short spur up onto Auchineden Hill. Here you should see ravens displaying and performing aerobatics in the updraughts.

126

Ravens

4. At the trig point on the top of the hill look round to enjoy the view, which now includes the Isle of Arran to the south-west and Glasgow, not very distant and enclosed in its valley to the south. Then follow one of the obvious wide paths to the left, heading for the left end of the Campsies, where you may be able to pick out Dumgoyne in front. One path leads to a cairn on the next high point, the other goes along the edge of the escarpment and by-passes the cairn. Carry on in the same direction, picking the best way. The ground is boggy but otherwise the walking is easy, and all paths eventually lead in the same direction. The conifer plantation seen on the way up appears in front and the path steepens and turns left to descend to the ladderstile. Cross and retrace your outward route to the car park.

Practicals

Type of walk: This is an exciting walk. It is fairly easy to traverse, although care must be taken in places where the ground is rough or slippery. Some boggy areas. The cliffs at the Whangie are quite slippery and very steep with recognised rock-climbing routes; they are not the place for children to play although they will love scrambling round the lower rocks.

Distance: 3 miles/5km
Time: 3 hours
Maps: OS Explorer 347, OS Landranger 64

33

Overtoun House and Doughnot Hill

Park either in the car park in front of Overtoun House or another, on the left, just before you reach the house, grid ref 424782. To reach this take the minor road, Milton Brae, heading north off the A82 one kilometre west of Dunglass roundabout, and just past two filling stations, one on either side of the road. Continue for a mile and then go on ahead through the gateway of Overtoun House.

Overtoun House was built for James White, later Lord Overtoun, a Glasgow businessman and factory owner. The house is a fine example of the 'Scots Baronial' style fashionable in the

Overtoun House

mid-nineteenth century, and has extensive grounds laid out with exotic trees and flowering plants collected from as far afield as the Himalayas. It was given to the people of Dumbarton in 1939 and has now been leased to a Christian group. Among other plans they intend to open a teashop here.

The bridge beside the house is dramatic. It was designed by Henry Ernest Milner, who also designed part of Princes Street Gardens. It spans the gorge of the Overtoun Burn; the burn itself has been altered in places to make it more romantic, introducing extra pools and little waterfalls. The hydro system which supplied Overtoun House with its electricity was one of the first to be built in Scotland. A pipe led from the artificial pond above the house down to the turbine house below **Spardie Linn**. The latter is a double fall about 10m high and is very fine when in spate.

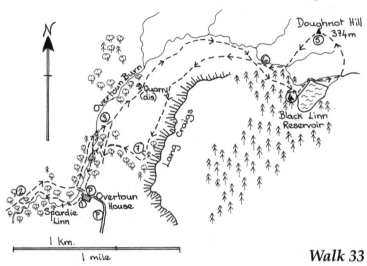

Walk 33

1. Walk in front of the house and turn left down steps before the bridge. Follow the path which continues downhill above the Overtoun Burn, first through rhododendrons on the edge of a lawn set about with fine specimen trees and then into woodland. Cross a wooden bridge over the burn, go up the bank and then carry on down steps, with the noise of Spardie Linn, loud in the enclosed space. At the foot of the steps look back through the trees to see the spectacular (when in spate) waterfall. A ruined building on the right of the path is all that remains of the turbine house. The cliffs are hung

129

with ferns and, in spring, bluebell, sanicle and wild garlic carpet the steep slopes. Ignore two stepped paths going off right and walk down the delightful gorge until a solid fence blocks the path. Turn right and climb steps to the surfaced drive above.

2. Turn right and walk gently uphill until you reach the bridge by Overtoun House once more. Take a clear path on the left before the bridge and walk up through the woods with the burn to your right. Ignore paths going down to bridges on the right and take a path which climbs left, following the estate wall, into tall pine and beech. Continue with the wall to your left until the path descends steps and begins to curl round to the right, towards the burn. Look for a narrow and sometimes muddy path, on the left, through rhododendrons and follow the fence at edge of the woodland. Cross the burn on a metal bridge over a water pipe and climb the steep slope ahead to a metal stile over the fence into a field.

3. Walk up the field, heading towards the end of the row of crags in front of you. When you reach a broad green path, a short way along, turn left and follow it across the open country. Wind round the right hand edge of old quarry workings, now overgrown and grassy, and on up the valley with the crags to the right and the burn, which has eroded the deep valley into shales with bands of white quartz, down to the left. The green path follows the line of the waterpipe seen earlier. In front, as you climb, the rounded knoll of Doughnot Hill comes into view. Go round the end of the crags to another metal stile and cross it into a forestry plantation. The path goes on along a rather wet and muddy ride; at intervals the dense spruce trees open up to give views out towards Doughnot Hill. Suddenly the trees end; climb the bank in front of you, which is a grassy dam, to look out over Black Linn reservoir.

4. Turn left to walk along the top of the dam, enjoying the open view. As you approach the far end, go down left to step over the reservoir outflow where it is narrow and cross the fence beyond. Follow the line of the fence up and round the corner to join a clear path going uphill from the reservoir corner. The path forks but the branches soon rejoin. A few metres beyond this junction the path winds right following a bend in a burn, and at this point look for another indistinct path going straight ahead through rushes. It soon becomes much more obvious and curls round onto the higher part of the moor heading for Doughnot Hill. In wet weather it will be boggy

Reed bunting

and you will have to pick your way with care. The final climb up Doughnot Hill is on short dry grass, and there is a sudden splendid view from the trig point on top. It embraces all points of the compass; Loch Lomond and its hills to the north, the Arrochar Alps, the Luss Hills, Cowal, the Clyde along to Dumbarton with Arran just peeping over the Renfrew Heights and Ailsa Craig showing through a gap, then the Galloway Hills, on round to the Campsies and the Forth Valley, and yet more mountains.

5. When you have had enough of the view, go back to the dam and through the forest to the stile. If, however, you found the walk over the moor too wet, you can easily vary the return by going down the grassy slopes of the hill, heading for the bottom corner of the plantation. As you go look for snipe and reed buntings. Step over the broken fences here and walk uphill just inside the forest fence with the trees on your left until you come down into a little hollow with a very steep slope on the far side. Here step over the fence again and follow an animal path round the hillside which brings you easily back up to the main path just outside the forest.

6. Turn right and go back down the path as it curves round a hollow and then round a small knoll. Then take a narrower path going off, left, up the next knoll, which winds delightfully in and out of the grassy hills and flats below the basalt crags, Lang Craigs. These tower up on your left and here kestrels nest and may be seen hovering on the updraughts. If the path becomes indistinct, keep to the tops of the ridges until it becomes clear again. Go down a grassy defile beside an old iron fence, cross a ruined wall and go on up onto a long ridge. There are trees below the crags now and from here there is a fine view of Dumbarton Rock on the Clyde.

7. Abruptly, the ridge ends. Zigzag down a clear path, turn right and descend the pasture, with a shelter belt of mature trees and rhododendrons on the left, until you meet a grassy track. Turn left, climb a padlocked gate or the fence beside it, and walk on down the track. Overtoun House is now in sight above the trees ahead. Take the first right, then where the path starts to go uphill, turn left and, at the next junction, left again. Walk along the side of the small pond, which was the reservoir for the hydro scheme, and turn left before the bridge over its outflow to go on down the side of the burn. Climb steps and turn left to walk up a lime avenue. At its end turn right onto the lawn in front of Overtoun House.

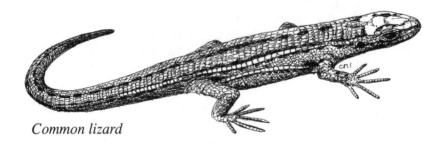

Common lizard

Practicals

Type of walk: This challenging walk is a surprise. It takes you through woods, beside streams and over the high moorland of the Kilpatrick Hills and feels quite remote, yet it is just behind Dumbarton The view from Doughnot Hill, known locally as The Doughnut, is stunning.

Distance: 6 miles/9.5km
Time: 3–4 hours
Maps: OS Explorer 347, OS Landranger 64

Balloch Castle

Park in the large car park behind Balloch Castle, grid ref 391832. To reach this enter the Country Park at the North Lodge and take the first turn on the right, leading to the parking area. To reach Balloch Castle take the A811 Balloch to Stirling road. Turn left at the roundabout after crossing the River Leven into Balloch and follow the signs.

At the end of the eighteenth century, John Buchanan of Ardoch, a wealthy Glasgow business man, bought **Balloch Estate** and commissioned architect Robert Lugar to build his new gothic-style mansion. Early in the 1900s Glasgow Corporation bought the estate and created Loch Lomond Park. It became a popular day trip for Glasgow people. In 1980 it became Balloch Castle Country Park and in 2002 it became the only country park in Scotland's first national park.

Balloch Castle

The *Maid of the Loch* was built by A.J. Inglis of Pointhouse, Glasgow, in 1953, and is now the sole surviving Loch Lomond paddle steamer and also the last traditional paddle steamer to have been built in the UK.

1. Walk down beside the outbuildings towards the castle, enjoying the many grey squirrels which frequent the car park and gardens and are extremely tame. Wander round the castle to admire the architecture and the views out over Loch Lomond, and make use of the excellent Visitor Centre at the back. Carry on along the drive, heading south, with fine lawns stretching away on your right and specimen trees on your left. At the end of the lawns keep on into the trees and then take a shady pathway curving away on your right. Follow it

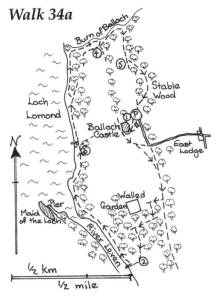

Walk 34a

until you can see the walls of the kitchen garden through the trees and then turn left into another pathway. The woods here are like tropical rainforest, huge specimen trees underlaid with bamboo and ferns. Turn right at a wider track and then left where there is a cycle-path sign. This path comes out into a car park, which you should cross diagonally to go through a gap in the wall to the right of a barrier.

2. Turn right and walk down the road beyond, to come to a slipway on the River Leven. Boats are moored all along the banks and mallards frequent the slipway. Turn right and go along above the riverbank, enjoying the busy scenes. The woods are wet and full of irises in flower in the summer, but the path is dry. The river, down to your left, gradually widens and the far bank curves away as you reach the lower end of Loch Lomond. Beyond the trees, on the far bank, you can see the old steamboat *Maid of the Loch*, now a restaurant.

134

3. At a junction of tracks carry straight on, along the middle one of three, towards a newly renovated boathouse and slipway. Go behind the boathouse, with views back up to Balloch Castle to your right, and continue above the shore. The path becomes narrower and goes back into woodland. At the next junction take the left branch, still just above the shore and walk on until you almost reach the fence at the end of the park.

Grey squirrel

Turn right here and walk up a delightful path beside a hurrying burn, with a steep bank on your right. There are little waterfalls in the burn and the banks are hung with ferns.

4. Suddenly the path makes a sharp hairpin bend, to the right and, just round this bend, a less obvious path goes off to the left, continuing the route up by the burn (this is called 'fairy glen'). Ascend the path which is a bit rough for the first few metres but soon improves. At a Y-junction take the right branch which goes uphill into beech trees. Cross the remains of an old wall and come out of the trees to walk along the top of a meadow. The path passes through a narrow belt of trees and then into another. An indistinct lane, Coo Lane, goes off here on the right and this does go back to the car park but it is overgrown and wet.

5. It is better to carry straight on across it and follow the narrow path which winds round inside the edge of Stable Wood, a fairly young and open woodland. The path brings you back down to join Coo Lane near its end. Turn left and follow it down to the main drive, just beyond the car park. Turn right to return to your car.

Practicals

Type of walk: A gentle stroll through a lovely park.

Distance: 2 ½ miles/4km
Time: 1–1 ½ hours
Maps: OS Explorer 347, OS Landranger 56

34b

Duncryne

Park in a layby at the entrance to Duncryne Wood, grid ref 433855. To reach this take the minor road leaving the A811 to the south-east at the north-east end of the village of Gartocharn.

Duncryne is a volcanic plug as are so many little hills in this area. There is no right of way to the little summit but the owners are happy for responsible walkers to go there, keeping to the paths provided. They hope you will enjoy their 'point of view'!

Ben Lomond from Duncryne

The cover illustration of this volume depicts the view over Loch Lomond from the top of Duncryne.

1. Go through a kissing gate and walk up the right edge of the pleasant deciduous wood. At the far end go through a gate to cross the field on a narrow way between fences, enjoying views through trees to the Luss Hills beyond Loch Lomond. Then go through another

kissing gate and turn right to begin the climb up the small but steep hill. At first there are mature oak trees but you soon emerge onto a bracken-covered hillside, which in May will be covered with bluebells.

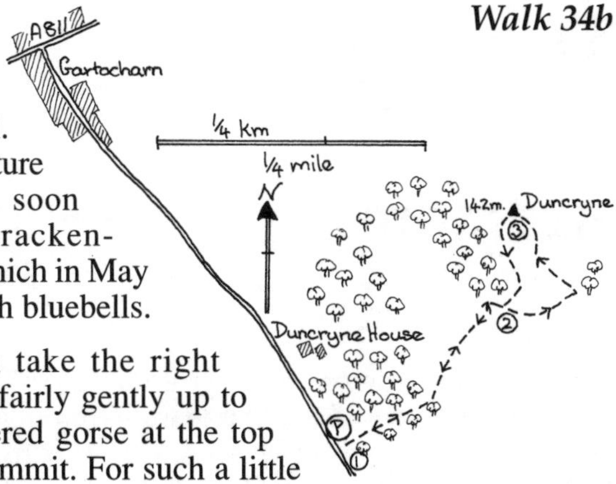

2. At the Y-junction take the right branch and zigzag fairly gently up to pass through scattered gorse at the top onto a small flat summit. For such a little effort there is an enormous reward; the view is stupendous. You are looking all the way up Loch Lomond.

3. When you have looked your fill, walk back away from the trig point and view, to descend by another path, which joins your path of ascent at the Y-junction mentioned earlier. Turn right and return across the field and through the wood to your car.

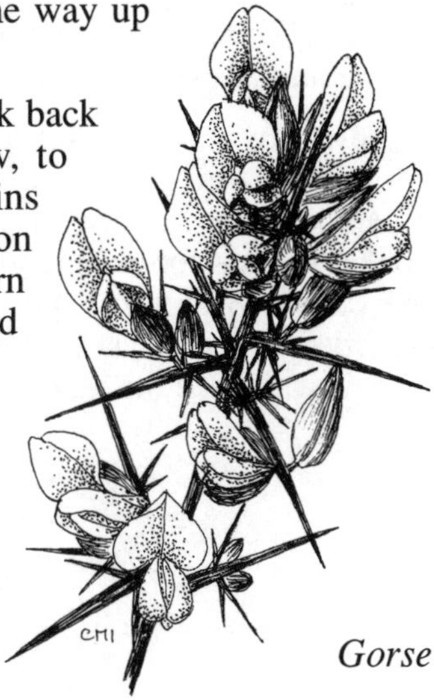

Gorse

Practicals

Type of walk: A short delectable ramble, with a magnificent view to be enjoyed for very little effort.

Distance: ½ mile/1km
Time: ½ hour
Maps: OS Explorer 347, OS Landranger 56

35

Ardmore

Park south of Ardmore farm, grid ref 323787. This is reached by following the A814 from Dumbarton, through Cardross and then Geilston. Once past the signs for Cardross Cemetery and Crematorium carry on for 500m to turn left immediately beyond a cottage. Drive on to cross the railway line and park overlooking the sandy shore of the Firth of Clyde, with Greenock, Port Glasgow and Gourock over the wide waterway.

Yairs are old fish traps, constructed of stone or wood that run perpendicular to the shoreline and curve, usually upstream, to form a bent arc. The fish swim in on the flood tide and are left in the pool as the tide ebbs; sometimes nets are fixed on the yair to increase the catch. Wooden stakes interwoven with wattle have been recorded in some cases. There are two you might spot, off shore, on this walk, see the map.

Lodge, Ardmore

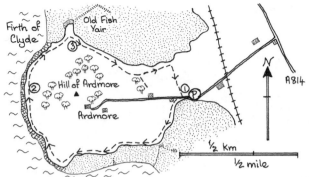

Walk 35

1. From the parking area walk on along the narrow road and at The Lodge join a track to the left of the dwelling. Go on along the pleasing track, with pasture (the haunt of skylarks) to the right and the waters of the Clyde to the left. Here you might spot waders on the shore. Then you can look across to the right over more pastures to Ardmore house on the side of the Hill of Ardmore. Wind on round on the good path and look inland to see a clump of wild cherry trees. Stroll past conglomerate rock on the beach and then large plates of sandstone. Go on to pass through gorse bushes; the colour and perfume of the blossom is delightful.

2. Look across the estuary to see Helensburgh and then follow the path as it continues along the edge of the shore. Look right to see the Hill of Ardmore framed with mixed deciduous trees, skirted by birch and pussy willow and hemmed with gorse. Carry on past patches of yellow iris and as the path winds east look left into the bay. If the tide is out you might spot an old fish yair, a permanent funnel-mouthed fish trap.

Yellow iris

139

Dunlin

3. Saunter on through a tunnel of gorse and then follow the path as it winds out into pasture at the head of the bay. Here take a path on the right, newly constructed and fenced, that takes you back to the Lodge. Walk on along the road to regain your vehicle.

Greenshank and black tailed godwits

Practicals

Type of walk: A short walk just right for a sunny evening stroll in summer or a brisk winter's walk. All the family including the dog will enjoy it.

Distance: 2 ¹/₄ miles/3.5km
Time: 1 ½ hours
Maps: OS Explorer 347, OS Landranger 63

Kilcreggan

Park above the ferry pier on the sea front at Kilcreggan, grid ref 242805. To reach this drive south from Garelochhead along the B833.

In 1882 the Rev. John Wilson, in *The Gazetteer of Scotland*, described **Kilcreggan** as

> a town on the south coast of Rosneath peninsula, Dumbartonshire. It stands opposite Gourock, 3 ½ miles north-west of Greenock; took its name from an ancient chapel long since extinct; has nearly all been built since 1840; is a much esteemed summer resort and watering place; consists chiefly of villas and ornate cottages on a stripe of coast upwards of a mile long.

It is still a delightful village, much esteemed and an attractive place from which to start a walk.

Kilcreggan

1. Cross the road from the sea front car park, above the pier, and take the steps opposite to follow the wide walled shady track as it ascends the steepish hill to Argyll Road. Cross and walk right to just beyond

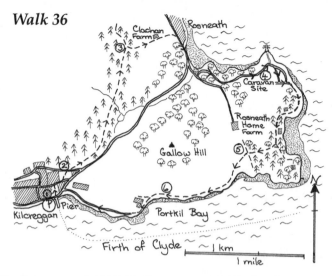

the last house on the left. A few steps on look for the easy-to-miss footpath up through the bluebell woodland, on your left. The path, generally distinct, winds through the trees and passes two small wet patches which can be avoided.

2. At Barbour Road, turn right and, in a few metres, cross to take the wide forest track, leading left away from the road. Stride the pleasing way with deciduous trees and bushes on either side, bounded by mossy walls with conifer plantations beyond. Carry on the gently climbing way. Follow the track as it begins to descend, with a fine view of Helensburgh on the other side of the lovely Gare Loch.

3. At the T-junction, turn right and descend steadily to a stile. Walk on to go through a gate to pass between Clachan farmhouse and its outbuildings and then continue down the lane to the B833. Cross and walk right, using the pavement and then a verge, to arrive at the side of Camsail Bay where there is more pavement. Where the B-road swings right and uphill, take the left branch, a 'no through road', and walk ahead. Keep left round the edge of the bay. At first the road is bordered by 3m high rhododendrons and then it passes through birch and oak bluebell woodland. The road ends at a caravan site and therefore, in the summer, it can be quite busy.

4. Pass through the caravans, walking past the reception block and turning right with the main road until you reach fenced pastureland.

142

Here turn left and walk on for a few metres to take a gate, on the right, into more delightful bluebell woodland. Continue on the wide track. Several little paths lead off left to the shore, where you might see curlew, redshank, hooded crow and shelduck in Culwatty Bay. Continue on the main track to pass two cottages, which have a grand view of the bay and then go on through a plantation. At the Y-junction, where there is a triangle of grass, bear right to walk a narrow road through tall conifers.

5. At the end of the woodland wind right to take a gated track on the left (almost opposite), which carries on through a fine open pasture. Pause here and look right to see the grand crenellated Rosneath Home farm. Over to the left, across the Firth of Clyde you can see Greenock and Port Glasgow. Carry on to go through a gated stile and soon wind right to walk the delectable way with the Firth of Clyde to your left and green pastures sloping gently up to gorse covered Gallow Hill, on your right.

6. Press on along the gated track with the Firth beside you, where eiders often idle. When the track turns inland, go ahead on a narrow path, above the shore and with the fence to your right. Continue on, soon to join a metalled road, which leads you back to the pleasing village of Kilcreggan.

Shelduck

Practicals

Type of walk: Pleasing walk from a pleasant small resort. Generally good tracks and paths. Some road walking, all of which requires care.

Distance: 6 miles/9.5km
Time: 3 hours
Maps: OS Explorer 347, OS Landranger 63 and 56

Beinn Dubh and Mid Hill from Luss

Park in the large car park at the north end of Luss, grid ref 359932. At the time of writing parking is free from the end of October to April, and on Sundays. In summer, there is a modest parking charge. Access the parking area from the A82, as it runs along Loch Lomond side, and then turn off into Luss village.

Luss is the place where St Kessog, an early Christian evangelist from southern Ireland, settled in the early part of the sixth century. He was apparently martyred here and legend has it that his body was embalmed in sweet herbs. After his burial the herbs grew and their scent pervaded the area and so it became known as Luss, from the Gaelic 'lus' for herb.

*Ram's
Head
Bridge,
Glen Luss*

The hardy Linton or **blackface sheep** were first introduced from the Borders into Glen Mollochan about 1747; this area has the longest history of intensive sheep rearing north of the Highland Line. At first they brought prosperity to an area otherwise marginal for farming, although overstocking and burning to increase the grass area soon led to a reduction in the fertility of the soil and an increase in unpalatable grasses and bracken.

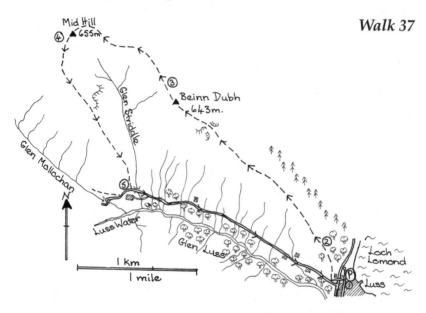

Walk 37

1. Turn left out of the car park and walk down the road to turn right just past the school, signposted 'Glen Luss'. Opposite the school entrance take a path on the left which goes up steps to cross the footbridge over the A82. Continue past a house and down its access track to a kissing gate. Beyond, turn right to take a stile into a field, and follow the clear path which soon leads into scattered oak woodland. Go past a telephone mast and on through a gate gap in a fence onto the open hill.

2. The grassy path runs up the main ridge very clearly and easily. The climb is relieved at intervals by relatively level shoulders; and the view across Loch Lomond to Ben Lomond is superb. If you turn round, all the lower island-studded part of Loch Lomond is spread below. Towards the top of the ridge rocky hollows appear, on the

right at first and then on both sides, and the path follows a line of old wooden fence posts. In wind the little hollows make good places to eat lunch. Come over the last rise and cross to Beinn Dubh's small summit cairn. Enjoy the stupendous view. Now you can see the Arrochar Alps in front, then the head of Loch Lomond surrounded by its dramatic hills and Ben Lomond towering over everything else. Here you might see ravens tumbling about in the air currents.

3. Walk ahead along the ridge with the fence posts now to your right and the contorted shape of the Cobbler in front. Where the fence turns off to the right keep straight ahead, along the crest of the hill, following the clear though narrower path. At a low col with peat hags the path vanishes; make your way across as best you can, trying to keep to the higher ground, and pick up the path again at the far side. Climb up towards Mid Hill, with a view of Glen Douglas and Inverbeg opening up on your right: the slopes below are rocky and precipitous, but the ridge continues broad and easy. Cross another small peat-hagged area and walk up to the summit cairn of Mid Hill.

4. Swing left to another cairn and then carry on down the ridge still following the narrow, distinct path. The highest of the Luss Hills, Doune Hill, is now to your right; Beinn Eich, with Beinn Caorach behind it, are ahead across Glen Mollochan. The slope gets steeper as you descend but is grassy and mainly dry underfoot. Meadow pipits abound, and if you are lucky you may see a hen harrier quartering the ground below for prey. You might also spot a fox. Descend to a stile over a fence and continue down the rough pasture beyond, winding round to the left to keep to drier high ground above the

Bluebells

146

bank of the Striddle Burn. Go down through a gate in the wall and again keep to the left of the field beyond, to arrive at another gate, which opens onto a metalled road by a large passing place.

5. Turn left on the road to walk down the glen. Notice the bridge over the Striddle Burn, which has a carved Ram's head on the downstream side to celebrate the prosperity brought to the glen by the coming of the sheep. The road is very quiet and narrow, passing through lovely open oak and birch and giving good views out towards Loch Lomond. After two miles look for the path on the left to take you back to the kissing gate and over the footbridge to Luss to return to your car.

Hen harrier

Practicals

Type of walk: Easy uphill walking with a path all the way, but it does go up to 655m so don't forget to take waterproofs, map and a compass, and to wear warm clothes and boots. No dogs.

Distance:	7 miles/11.2km
Time:	5 hours
Maps:	OS Explorer 364, OS Landranger 56

38

Cruach Tairbeart

Park in the public car park, opposite the garage, at the head of Loch Long, grid ref 298049. This is reached by the A83.

This walk makes a fine circuit from the north end of Arrochar at the head of Loch Long. It traverses deciduous woodland and comes nearly to the west shore of Loch Lomond above the village of Tarbet. The word **Tarbet** (or Tarbert) means a low area where boats could be dragged across. It was over this isthmus that Magnus, son-in-law of King Haakon of Norway, carried his galleys. In this way he surprised the people living on Loch Lomond who thought they were quite safe from oversea raiders.

Arrochar

1. From the car park cross the busy A-road and walk south (right) to pass Loch Long Hotel. Just beyond, take the signposted Glen Loin footpath. Climb quite steeply, away from the road, up the zigzagging path through delightful bluebell woodland. At the T-junction turn right on a rising track, with yellow waymarks, in the direction of Arrochar and Tarbet station. Enjoy the views down to the loch, on

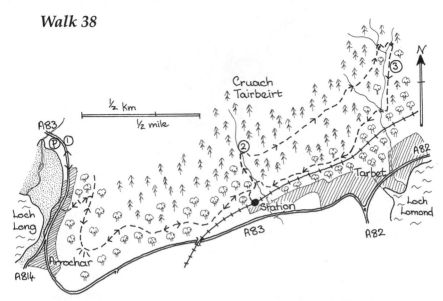

your right, with Beinn Narnain and The Cobbler towering above. After levelling for a short distance the path rises again to a viewpoint and a seat, then swings round to the left towards Loch Lomond. As you continue on you might be able to spot Ben Lomond. Pass through a barrier across the track and go on along the now roller-coaster path. Ignore the right turn to the station and then ascend below magnificent beech trees, following the red ringed marker posts. Wind round left and climb steadily for 200m with a burn to your right, ignoring the path which crosses the burn and goes down the far side—this is your return route.

2. Cross the burn at the ford and wind right and then left to continue on the pleasing path, now with conifers on either side and still on the red marker route. Soon you reach a clearing on the right, giving you a first view of Loch Lomond. Soon after you have an almost full length view of the loch. Then make a loop round a wet area and carry on along the red waymarked way through more conifers. Press on down to a wooden bridge over a burn and, on the far side, pass a picnic table up on the left. Carry on down the path with a ravine to your right, which steadily deepens.

3. After descending some more you have another good view of Loch Lomond. Go on to wind down right to cross another wooden footbridge and curve left, following the track with conifers to the

Coal tit

right and fine deciduous woodland to the left. Descend through a heavily mossed and lichened wall. Soon you can see the West Highland railway line to your left and then the path comes close beside it. Go on the lovely way to wind right, with the burn to your left. Climb a short distance to ford the hurrying water (this is the crossing you ignored on the way up) and then turn left to descend and wind right. Carry on. Ignore the turn down to the station and follow your outward route to return to the parking area on the loch.

Practicals

Type of walk: A really delightful walk, with good views and through lovely woodland. Good walking underfoot all the way. Suitable for all the family.

Distance: 4 ½ miles/7.2km
Time: 2 ½ hours
Maps: OS Explorer 364, OS Landranger 56

Ben Vorlich

Park on the broad hard verge on the east side of the A82, grid ref 322148, just north of Stuckendroin farm.

Ben Vorlich is a Munro at 3090ft/943m. It is one of the Arrochar Alps, slightly separated from the others by the trough containing Loch Sloy. It is unusual in that there is no agreed 'best' way to climb it, which means that no way is particularly over-used and eroded. The paths walked are pleasant and narrow.

Loch Sloy, seen well from the summit ridge of Ben Vorlich, is a hydro-electric dam. The water is piped to storage reservoirs above Inveruglas on Loch Lomondside and descends through huge pipes to the turbine house.

Lochan on Ben Vorlich

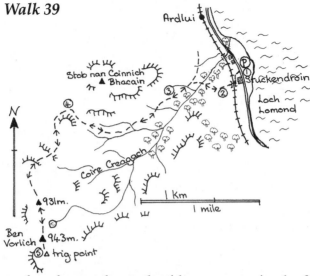

1. Walk south and cross the road, with care, opposite the farm. Go through the entrance gate and then the kissing gate, on the right, signposted 'Little Hills and Ben Vorlich'. Follow the waymarks along the right-hand edge of a field, with a fence on the left and a wall on the right. At the next waymark turn left and go along the top edge of the field to a gate leading to an underpass beneath the railway. Beyond the railway, go through another gate also signed Ben Vorlich. Remember to shut all gates as requested.

2. Walk ahead up a damp valley. Then climb to the left, out of the valley, and carry on up the drier edge of it into open woodland. Soon a burn appears below you. Here, descend to cross it on stones as soon as possible before the banks become too steep. Climb the far bank to cross a fence and continue uphill until you meet a clearer contouring path, where you turn left and go on through scattered birch to a stile in an electric fence.

3. Beyond the stile, climb steeply then cross a level area and ascend a rocky knoll to reach a burn. Turn right here, climb a ladder and cross the burn on a small fenced dam. Follow the level track beyond the dam for a short distance and then take a slightly less clear path, on the right, to climb the hillside, with another burn coming into view on the left. At a fork take the distinct right branch, which takes you across a heathery, peaty corrie floor. Then climb the continuing stony path to gain the ridge.

4. Cross to the far side of the ridge, which is broad here and covered with rocky hillocks. Follow the clear path as it winds in and out between them, climbing steadily. There are two places where the path goes over a rock slab but both are easy-angled and provided with plenty of footholds. When you need a rest, pause to admire the splendid views and keep a keen watch for a golden eagle or a raven. Cross a small top and then walk along the pleasant ridge to the summit; the large cairn which you reach first is the actual summit, the trig point further on is a little lower. There is a delightful lochan cradled below the summit in a high corrie.

Golden eagle

5. To return, retrace your steps.

Practicals

Type of walk: This is a delightful climb in good weather, and makes a pleasing contrast with Ben Lomond on the other side of the loch in that it is much less frequented. It is not a climb for a bad or misty day because the paths are narrow and the summit ridge is complex and can be confusing in poor visibility. Therefore unless you are proficient with a compass and a map make sure you choose a clear day. No dogs.

Distance: 7 miles/11.4km
Time: 5 hours
Maps: OS Explorer 364, OS Landranger 56

40

Ben Glas falls

Ask to park in the huge car park behind the Drovers' Inn, grid ref 318185, where you will want to be a customer after your walk. To reach the inn, take the A82 to Inverarnan at the head of Loch Lomond.

The Drovers' Inn at Inverarnan as its name suggests was used by drovers. They brought cattle over the Lairig Arnan from Glen Fyne and carried on over the drove road, used in this walk, to Glen Gyle and then to markets at Crieff. From the 1880s the inn became a favourite centre for climbers.

Glen Falloch has also been a through route not only as a drove road but also as the route of a military road built after the 1745 uprising and then in 1894 the

Part of Ben Glas Falls in ice

West Highland railway was built through the glen. Today the rail-way is still there but the occasional noise of a train is drowned by the traffic noise from the improved A82 road. The West Highland Way (WHW) also goes through the glen. Once away from the im-mediate vicinity of the road the noise is not too intrusive.

Ben Glas Burn plunges nearly 300m in 1km over a series of fine falls which are spectacular after rain. The best view is from Inverarnan across the valley, but the views of the upper falls obtained on this walk are well worth the effort.

1. From Inverarnan walk north along the footpath beside the A82 until you reach the footbridge over the River Falloch which gives access to Beinglas farm. Cross the bridge and turn right immediately as directed by the WHW signpost. Follow the riverbank and then the bank of the Ben Glas Burn, looking out for dippers, until you reach the footbridge over the burn behind the farm. Do NOT cross but turn left and almost immediately take a small path on the right which climbs very steeply up beside the Ben Glas burn, here a series of waterfalls in a deep ravine. The path zigzags up the hill through scattered trees to a fence gap followed by a stile over a deer fence.

Walk 40

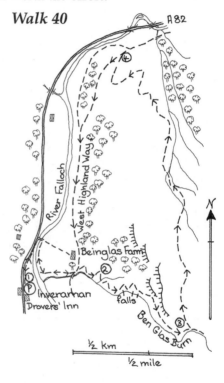

2. Continue climbing beyond the fence, with the waterfalls invisible away to the right. As you get higher you will reach a place where there is a small but distinct path on the right along a shelf from which you can see the higher falls on the burn. They are splendid. Do NOT attempt to see them before this point, because the hillside is precipitous. A little higher and a deer fence appears on your

right; the path curves round beside it and then climbs up to another stile, where the fence leaves the burn and runs across the hillside. Continue to zigzag up before contouring right and finally climbing over a shoulder to a level ridge above the burn. In front is a wide bleak upland valley, Ben Glas to the left and Beinn Chabhair ahead, with the burn in a deep channel running through it. The path runs along above the burn.

3. Follow the path until it turns right beside the burn as it flows down from the moorland basin. Here take a clear track on the left, an old drove road over to Glen Gyle from Glen Falloch. Follow it as it climbs gently to curve round a hillock on the left below Ben Glas and go on where it winds down the wide hillside beyond, giving fine views up Glen Falloch to Ben Lui, Beinn Oss and Beinn Dubhchraig, and the Mamlorn Hills. Soon birch trees appear, softening the view. Swing left by a burn and follow the widening zigzags until the track joins the WHW by a superb ancient holly tree with four trunks.

4. Turn left and walk down the WHW. The track passes into woodland, which is beginning to regenerate now that there is a deer fenced enclosure above on the left. The views down Glen Falloch to Beinn Vorlich are superb. Here you might see woodcock in the woodland. At Beinglas farm follow the WHW markers round across the back of the buildings to join your outward path. Turn right and retrace your steps to Inverarnan and the inn.

Practicals

Type of walk: This is a short but very steep walk. It climbs $^1/_3$ of the way up Beinn Chabhair, a Munro, and is nothing like an easy stroll. Be prepared. In winter the path by the waterfall can be covered in ice and very treacherous. No dogs are allowed on this walk. Shooting information, 01499 600137.

Distance:	4 miles/6.5km
Time:	3–4 hours
Maps:	OS Explorer 364, OS Landranger 56 and on 50

Woodcock roding

Falls of Falloch

If you are not tired after the climb by Ben Glas waterfalls, drive two miles north up Glen Falloch and park in the car park on the right at grid ref 334208. Walk north from the parking area along a path parallel with the road and then turn right down steps through the lovely oak woodland to the side of River Falloch. The river seethes over rock ridges and through potholes, and a very short distance upstream is the splendid waterfall, 10m high, with a deep basin below known (inevitably) as Rob Roy's Bathtub. To return go up left at the side of the basin and follow the top path back to the car park.

Falls of Falloch

Clan Walks

A series of walks described by Mary Welsh, covering some of the most popular holiday areas in the Scottish Highlands and Islands.

Titles published so far include:

1. 44 WALKS ON THE ISLE OF ARRAN
2. WALKING THE ISLE OF SKYE
3. WALKS IN WESTER ROSS
4. WALKS IN PERTHSHIRE
5. WALKS IN THE WESTERN ISLES
6. WALKS IN ORKNEY
7. WALKING SHETLAND
8. WALKING THE ISLES OF ISLAY, JURA AND COLONSAY
9. WALKS ON CANNA, RUM, EIGG AND MUCK
10. WALKS ON TIREE, COLL, COLONSAY AND A TASTE OF MULL
11. WALKING DUMFRIES AND GALLOWAY
12. WALKS IN ARGYLL AND BUTE
13. WALKING DEESIDE, DONSIDE AND ANGUS
14. WALKING THE TROSSACHS, LOCH LOMONDSIDE AND THE CAMPSIE FELLS
15. WALKING GLENCOE, LOCHABER AND THE GREAT GLEN

OTHER TITLES IN PREPARATION

Books in this series can be ordered through booksellers anywhere. In the event of difficulty write to Clan Books, The Cross, DOUNE, FK16 6BE, Scotland.